DINNER

WITH

Dickens

DINNER

WITH

Dickens

RECIPES INSPIRED BY THE LIFE AND WORK
OF CHARLES DICKENS

PEN VOGLER

CICO BOOKS

LONDON NEW YORK

*To the memory of my beloved
father, Jon, and to my niece
Laura and my nephew Julian,
who made testing recipes such fun.*

Published in 2017 by CICO Books
An imprint of Ryland Peters & Small Ltd
20–21 Jockey's Fields, London WC1R 4BW
341 E 116th St, New York, NY 10029
www.rylandpeters.com

10 9 8 7 6 5 4 3 2 1

Editor: Gillian Haslam
Designer: Vicky Rankin
Photographer: Ria Osborne
Stylist: Luis Peral
Food stylist: Ellie Jarvis

Art director: Sally Powell
Head of production: Patricia Harrington
Publishing manager: Penny Craig
Publisher: Cindy Richards

NOTES:

All eggs are US large/UK medium unless otherwise
specified.

Both American (imperial and US cups) and British
(metric) measurements are included in these recipes for
your convenience. However, it is important to work with
only one set of measurements and not alternate between
the two within a recipe.

CONTENTS

INTRODUCTION

The great Victorian thinker Thomas Carlyle, much admired by Charles Dickens, wrote that money was "the universal sole nexus of man to man" (*Chartism*, 1839). It became a key insight for the vertiginously changing social and economic landscape of Victorian England. Born in 1812, Dickens was fascinated by what connected people, and he dramatizes the material relationship described by Carlyle through the food his characters give, share, steal, or long for. Every beefsteak pudding, morsel of pickled salmon, or sip of currant wine tells us something about the giver, the receiver, and the relationship between them in terms of their moral, economic, or social life.

The wealthy Dombey and his servants alike guzzle but don't value a luscious wedding breakfast. The feckless Mr. Micawber, modeled on Dickens' own father, instantly forgets his despair at his latest economic mishap (his water supply is cut off) when he makes punch for David Copperfield. The Cratchit family will have goose for Christmas dinner, no matter how benighted their finances, until the reformed Scrooge makes them a gift of the then much rarer luxury—a turkey. Pip, by stealing food for the convict Magwitch in *Great Expectations*, unwittingly forges a lifelong economic relationship with him.

Childhood hunger haunts Dickens' work. Thanks to the biography written shortly after his death by his close friend John Forster, we now know that the twelve-year-old Charles Dickens was hurtled into self-sufficiency when his father was imprisoned in the London debtors' prison, the Marshalsea. His wife and the younger children went with him—a scenario vividly re-created in *Little Dorrit*. Charles was sent to work pasting labels onto boot-blacking in a rat-infested factory near London's Charing Cross. His autobiographical novel *David Copperfield* shows not just the desperation of having an empty belly, but also the ache for the consolation and security of being nourished by a loving parent.

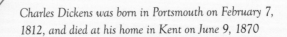

Charles Dickens was born in Portsmouth on February 7, 1812, and died at his home in Kent on June 9, 1870

The mother-figure, who should feed and nurture her child, is deformed throughout Dickens' novels, probably because the writer could never forget —or forgive—that, even after his father was released from prison, his mother wanted him to continue working for an income rather than attend school. So we laugh at Mrs. Jellyby, who serves her guests a virtually raw dinner as her children tumble downstairs in *Bleak House*, and the empty-headed Mrs. Nickleby who, instead of offering direction to her children for their difficulties, whimsically recollects the "roast pig, with sage and onion sauce, and made gravy" of a happier past.

Dickens' work shows that he saw domestic comfort and virtue as the answer to many of society's ills. He became part of a Victorian movement of reformers and worked with the philanthropic heiress Angela Burdett-Coutts, particularly in setting up a home to teach fallen women cookery and other domestic virtues. He admired Henry Mayhew, an advocate of social reform whose reports on *London Labour and the London Poor* are real-life counterparts of Dickens' descriptions of the very poorest and those who are abused or forgotten by the organizations who should protect them. Jo, the crossing sweeper in *Bleak House*, eats dirty bread while sitting on the doorstep of a religious society, and is rescued at last by the kindness of individuals. *A Christmas Carol*—possibly the most influential of Dickens' books—places food and family at the center of the celebration. Its view of Christmas as a time of feasting and enjoyment in the home, rather than in the church or wider community, has set the tone for Christmas ever since.

Dickens made his middle-class readers see that the welfare systems they supported didn't feed children, but starved them. Oliver Twist is punished and sold, like a slave, for daring to ask for more gruel. The adults whose job is to care for him are lesser moral beings than the thieves he falls in with. Fagin and his urchins give Oliver a supper of sausages, somewhere to sleep, and breakfast of coffee, hot rolls, and "ham which the Dodger had brought home in the crown of his hat," although Dickens' choice of food is troublingly un-kosher.

Dickens' scenes of eating are always balanced, to show us something about sharing and isolation, generosity and greed. Daniel Quilp, in *The Old Curiosity Shop*, disturbs his downtrodden wife's attempts at sociable, comfortable teas with her friends. He, eating alone, is sub-human as he consumes hard-boiled eggs with their shells, prawns with their heads, and boiling tea. *Nicholas Nickleby*'s vicious schoolmaster, Wackford Squeers, who congratulates himself on denying food to his poor charges, is balanced by the blunt Yorkshireman John Browdie, who reveals his good-heartedness through his pleasure in watching hungry people eat.

As Dickens established himself professionally—initially as a political reporter, then, with the success of his first book, *The Pickwick Papers*, as a writer of fiction—sharing food became a crucial part of his own life, and its moral purpose is mirrored in his books. Being able to enjoy and share food and drink was a human right for everybody, rich and poor alike. He had no time for the temperance movements, whose aim was to deprive the poor of much-needed enjoyment.

Dickens delighted in sharing food with friends. His correspondence is littered with notes inviting people to dine at prompt hours—"at ¼ before 7 o'clock." His dinner table was rich with conversation from actors, writers, and thinkers of the day, including Thomas and Jane Carlyle, Leigh Hunt, Elizabeth Gaskell, Henry Wadsworth Longfellow, and Harriet Beecher Stowe.

Catherine Dickens, despite the stresses of pregnancy and motherhood (she gave birth to ten children), threw herself into catering for her husband's demanding social palate. In 1851 she published a little book, *What Shall We Have for Dinner?*, with pages of menus, "bills of fare" for different sizes of dinner party and different seasons, and a short appendix of recipes. We can surmise from this which dishes were popular with Dickens and his family. The recurrence of mutton, oysters, shrimp, raspberries, salad, macaroni, and cock-a-leekie soup on the menus all hint at Charles' love of the sea, Catherine's Scottish origins, and their European travels.

It must have been difficult for Catherine to carve out a domestic niche for herself, and it is impressive that she did so with this book. Long after her death in 1879, her eldest son, Charley—the only one of her children to live with Catherine after Dickens forced their separation in 1858—commented, "The critics with one accord agreed that the little work was well enough, but that no man could possibly survive the consumption of such frequent toasted cheese" ("Reminiscences of My Father" in *Windsor Magazine*, Christmas supplement, 1934).

This book celebrates the food of nineteenth-century England by re-creating some of the meals and dishes that Dickens describes in his novels, and some real-life occasions that we know he enjoyed with family and friends. Many of the dishes are suggested by Catherine Dickens' book, and the recipes come from books of the day we know she used. Margaret Dods was a pseudonym for the Scottish writer and editor Christian Isobel Johnstone, and Catherine's Scottish mother would certainly have used her *Cook and Housewife's Manual*. Catherine also took recipes directly from Alexis Soyer and the American writer Sarah Josepha Hale. We know that the excellent Eliza Acton read Dickens (she names one of her recipes—Ruth Pinch's Beefsteak Pudding—after the character in *Martin Chuzzlewit*), and I have drawn gratefully on Acton's work. I have also used traditional recipes from Hannah Glasse and John Farley from the mid-eighteenth century, and newer ideas from Mrs. Beeton and Mrs. A.B. Marshall and other cookbooks published toward the end of the Victorian era to give a sense of the wide sweep of taste across this rapidly changing century.

I hope that *Dinner with Dickens* shows that Dickens wrote about the food and cooking of his time not just for dramatic and social effect, but also because it was comforting, nutritious, delicious, and often great fun. Victorian food has a reputation for being either stodgy or unnecessarily fussy, but I hope this book shows that much of it was delicious and attractive.

Every recipe here has been tested and updated for modern cooks, but I have learned a great deal from our Victorian forebears. They can teach us much about avoiding waste and being economical, such as using molasses (treacle) to give brown soda bread a depth of taste and great keeping properties. They show us surprising combinations of ingredients, such as using oysters or other seafood to bring out the depth of flavor in lamb or mutton, or adding ground cloves and lemon to make the best gingerbread ever. Victorian food can look spectacular and also taste fresh and delicate. A Charlotte Russe demands a whole afternoon of preparation, but it is great fun to make and, with fresh berries, cream, and homemade sponge fingers, it is beautifully light and fruity. And we can turn to Victorians to discover tricks for using old-fashioned ingredients, such as bone marrow that turns a bread-and-butter pudding into something rich, toffeeish, and rather heavenly.

I have included a recipe for gruel, but nobody will blame you for bypassing it and trying instead almond cake, cod and oyster sauce, or a savory pork pie. I hope you will enjoy cooking the dishes as much as I have and that, like Oliver Twist, your family and guests will be back for more.

CHAPTER 1

A Yorkshire Breakfast

Nicholas Nickleby

— ◆ —

The Yorkshire Schoolmaster at "The Saracen's Head"
H.K. Browne (Phiz)

Dickens, though rooted in London and Kent, was also concerned with specific issues in the north of England, and went to Yorkshire to investigate its infamous boarding schools, which were widely used to offload unwanted wards or offspring at little expense. In *Nicholas Nickleby* he drew on a real example to portray the

schoolmaster Squeers and Dotheboys Hall (with its advertised promise of "No extras, no vacations, and diet unparalleled"). Squeers is first seen tucking into coffee, cold beef, and toast for breakfast at the Saracen's Head in London, while meting out a brief swallow of watered-down milk to the small boys in his charge. "Subdue your appetites my dears, and you've conquered human nature," he tells them, voicing the popular notion that to starve children was part of a moral crusade, which therefore legitimized neglect and exploitation. In Yorkshire, Dickens also met people of big hearts—and appetites—and he contrasts Squeers with the kindly Yorkshireman John Browdie. Breakfasting at the same inn later in the tale, Browdie complains that the pigeon pies are too light (containing as they do only three pigeons and a trifling matter of steak in each, "and a crust so loight that you doan't know when it's in your mooth and when it's gane"). Browdie enjoys his food but, unlike Squeers, he also delights in watching other hungry people eat.

A hearty breakfast of beef, ham, and piles of Yorkshire cake is offered to Sim Tappertit in *Barnaby Rudge*. The Browdies have a similarly magnificent start to the day, as Nicholas discovers when he returns to Yorkshire and finds them at "vast mounds of toast, new-laid eggs, boiled ham, Yorkshire pie, and other cold substantials." As these quantities of toast and eggs show, Victorian breakfasts were beginning to feature dishes that were distinct from those of other meals, but ham, beef, and pies were still enjoyed, by those who could afford them, at any time of day, including breakfast-time.

The Browdies' breakfast is all "admirably adapted to the cold bleak morning," unlike Mrs. Squeers' housekeeping: the "diet unparalleled" she gives her pathetic charges is brimstone (sulfur) and treacle for breakfast, to ruin their appetites and make them cheaper to feed.

Mrs. Browdie apologizes to Nicholas that he has found them eating in the kitchen together, rather than the parlor. It is a comfortable scene with something already a little old-fashioned about it. Designated "breakfast rooms" were introduced at the end of the eighteenth century, when breakfast started to be a meal with its own characteristics. Mr. Dombey is wealthy enough to have one, but the Browdies do not have such an aspirational luxury.

YORKSHIRE CAKES

Sim Tappertit in *Barnaby Rudge* has a hearty breakfast of ham and beef and "sundry towers of buttered Yorkshire cake, piled slice upon slice in most alluring order." When he sees his host kissing his daughter, Sim is so jealous he hopes the Yorkshire cake will choke him. William Kitchiner's recipe uses a "sponge and dough" method that is still used for brioche and some French breads.

MAKES 12 CAKES

¼ oz/7g fresh yeast or ½ teaspoon/2.5g quick action dry yeast

⅔ cup/150ml milk

3¼ cups/450g strong all-purpose/plain flour

½ teaspoon salt

½ cup/120g butter

2 eggs

To have these ready for breakfast, start the previous evening.

If using fresh yeast, dissolve it in the milk. If using dried yeast, heat the milk in a saucepan until it is warm (but not hot) and sprinkle the dried yeast on top.

Place 1¾ cups/250g of the flour in a bowl, make a well in the center, and pour in the yeast mixture. Whisk to get a smooth batter. Cover with a clean dish towel and leave to rise for about 8–10 hours or overnight in a cool place.

In the morning, sprinkle the salt into the remaining flour and rub in the butter.

Whisk the eggs into the yeast mixture using a wooden spoon. It will look as if it has separated, but don't worry—as you slowly mix in the flour and butter mixture, it will all come together. Add more flour or more milk as necessary, to get a stiff dough.

Divide the dough into 12 equal pieces. Put them on an oiled baking tray, flattening them slightly, and cover with oiled plastic wrap/clingfilm or a wet dish towel. Let them rise in a warm place until doubled in size (anything from 1 to 2 hours, depending on the warmth of your room). Toward the end of the rising time, preheat the oven to 400°F/200°C/Gas 6.

Remove the plastic wrap/clingfilm and bake for about 15 minutes until golden brown. Eat warm and buttered.

NB To turn these into tea cakes, add ¼ cup/50g granulated/caster sugar and ⅓ cup/50g currants to the flour and butter mixture, after rubbing in the butter.

YORKSHIRE CAKES

*Take a pint and a half of Milk quite warm, a quarter of a pint of thick Small-Beer-
Yeast; mix them well together in a pan with sufficient Flour to make a thick Batter,
let it stand in a warm place covered over till it has risen as high as it will, rub six ounces
of Butter into some Flour till it is quite fine,- then break three eggs into your pan with
the Flour and Butter; mix them well together, then add sufficient flour to make it into
a Dough, and let it stand a quarter of an hour, then work it up again, and break
it into pieces about the size of an egg, or larger, as you may fancy, – roll them round
and smooth with your hand, and put them on tins, and let them stand covered over
with a light piece of flannel.*

WILLIAM KITCHINER, *Apicius Redivivus, or The Cook's Oracle*, 1817

A YORKSHIRE CHRISTMAS PIE

The appetite of the bluff Yorkshireman John Browdie is a running joke in *Nicholas Nickleby.* The breakfast that Nicholas shares with him on a winter morning includes "Yorkshire pie, and other cold substantials." Yorkshire pies were made at Christmas, often as gifts, and featured birds of a succession of sizes, from turkey down to partridge, boned and stuffed inside each other. Few modern ovens are big enough for this, but the recipe is fascinating.

A YORKSHIRE CHRISTMAS-PYE

First make a good Standing Crust, let the Wall and Bottom be very thick, bone a Turkey, a Goose, a Fowl, a Partridge, and a Pigeon, season them all very well, take half an Ounce of Mace, half an Ounce of Nutmegs, a quarter of an Ounce of Cloves, half an Ounce of black Pepper, all beat fine together, two large Spoonfuls of Salt, mix them together.

Open the Fowls all down the Back, and bone them; first the Pigeon, then the Partridge, cover them; then the Fowl, then the Goose, and then the Turkey, which must be large; season them all well first, and lay them in the Crust, so as it will look only like a whole Turkey; then have a Hare ready cased, and wiped with a clean Cloth. Cut it to Pieces, that is jointed; season it, and lay it as close as you can on one Side; on the other Side Woodcock, more Game, and what Sort of wild Fowl you can get. Season them well, and lay them close; put at least four Pounds of Butter into the Pye, then lay on your Lid, which must be a very thick one, and let it be well baked. It must have a very hot Oven, and will take at least four Hours.

This Pye will take a Bushel of Flour; in this Chapter, you will see how to make it. These Pies are often sent to London in a Box as Presents; therefore the Walls must be well built.

HANNAH GLASSE, *The Art of Cookery Made Plain and Easy,* 1747

BREAKFAST EGGS

The "new-laid eggs" at Nicholas's Yorkshire breakfast couldn't be taken for granted in the days before food regulations. Mrs. Beeton tests for freshness by touching them with the tongue (they will be warm) or holding them to a candle (they will be translucent). She also informs us that the shepherds of Egypt cooked them by whirling them around in their slings.

Preheat the oven to 425°F/220°C/Gas 7.

Thickly butter a small gratin dish and break in one or two eggs per person. Season with salt and a little white or black pepper. Dot with butter, and bake in the preheated oven for about 8 minutes for a soft yolk, 10 minutes for a set one.

Variations: put slices of hand-carved ham or smoked salmon or truffle shavings (not "truffle oil," which is nearly always fake) in the bottom of the dish, or a few freshly chopped herbs on top with the butter, such as parsley, chives, lovage, or tarragon.

OEUFS AU PLAT OR AU MIRROIR

Ingredients. 4 eggs, 1 oz. of butter, pepper and salt to taste.

Mode. Butter a dish rather thickly with good fresh butter; melt it, break the eggs into it the same as for poaching, sprinkle them with white pepper and fine salt, and put the remainder of the butter, cut into very small pieces, on the top of them. Put the dish on a hot plate, or in the oven, or before the fire, and let it remain until the whites become set, but not hard, when serve immediately, placing the dish they were cooked in on another. To hasten the cooking of the eggs, a salamander may be held over them for a minute; but great care must be taken that they are not too much done. This is an exceedingly nice dish, and one very easily prepared for breakfast.

Time, 3 minutes. Average cost, 5d.

Sufficient for 2 persons. Seasonable at any time.

MRS. BEETON'S *Book of Household Management*, 1861

YARMOUTH BLOATERS

Yarmouth bloaters are smoked herrings from the Norfolk seaside resort of Great Yarmouth, on England's east coast. Kept whole or "bloated" when cured, they are milder and moister than kippers. Francatelli recommends them as an "appetiser for Breakfast" and the malevolent Quilp, who crunches prawn- and egg-shells and cutlery, breakfasts on them whole. Peggotty, in *David Copperfield*, is "proud to call herself a Yarmouth Bloater." Catherine sometimes offered them as a savory at the end of a meal.

1 bloater per person

butter, to serve

Bloaters are smoked with their guts inside; if they haven't been gutted when you buy them, cut off the head and tail, split them down the belly, and pull out the innards. Keep the roe, if any, to serve on toast.

Slash the skin diagonally so they cook rapidly, then broil/grill them under a high heat for 2–3 minutes on each side.

Serve them, as Francatelli says, with fresh butter and a captain's biscuit (see page 84). As with all oily smoked fish, they go well with poached eggs and hot toast for breakfast. Horseradish sauce would be a good supper accompaniment.

YARMOUTH BLOATERS

Cut off the head and tail, split the bloater down the back, spread it out flat, and broil it on both sides over a clear sharp fire; send to table with a pat of fresh butter and a thick Captain's biscuit made hot in the oven or before the fire.

CHARLES ELME FRANCATELLI, *The Cook's Guide and Housekeeper's and Butler's Assistant*, 1861

~ BROWN BREAD ~

Brown, white, buttered... bread is significant throughout *Nicholas Nickleby*.
Nicholas and Kate worry frequently how they will "earn their bread" and
Nicholas amuses John Browdie by "powderin' awa' at the thin bread an'
butther!," a luxury Squeers denies the little boys in his care, who are given
instead a "minute wedge of brown bread;" still better than gruel. Brown soda
bread became popular in Irish and northern families toward the end of the
nineteenth century, when the new raising agents available meant bread could
be made almost instantly.

MAKES 1 LOAF

butter, for greasing

3¼ cups/450g wholemeal flour

1 teaspoon salt

**1 level teaspoon baking soda/
bicarbonate of soda**

**1½–1¾ cups/350–400ml
buttermilk (or milk mixed with
2 teaspoons lemon juice)**

**2 dessertspoons molasses/black
treacle**

Preheat the oven to 400°F/200°C/Gas 6. Butter a 1-lb/450-g loaf
pan/tin or a baking tray, depending on whether you want a loaf or
a cake shape.

Combine the flour, salt, and soda in a bowl and make a well in
the middle.

Whisk together the milk and molasses/treacle. Pour most of it into
the well and stir together well to combine, adding as much as you
need to get a soft, sticky dough. Either turn the dough quickly into
the loaf pan/tin or flour your hands and shape it into a round on
the baking tray, cutting a cross on the top with a sharp knife.

Bake in the preheated oven for 30–40 minutes until the crust is firm
and the loaf sounds hollow when tapped underneath.

BAKED BROWN BREAD

*1lb wheat meal, 1lb Indian corn meal, half a cup of treacle, salt, one egg, two teaspoonfuls
of baking soda, two teaspoonfuls of cream of tartar, milk or water.*

*Mode Mix wheat meal, Indian meal, half teaspoonful salt, baking soda, cream of tartar,
well together; warm the treacle, and add it with the milk (or water) to the dry ingredients.
Put in floured tin, and bake five hours in a moderate oven.*

MARTHA H. GORDON, *Cookery for Working Men's Wives*, 1888

CHAPTER 2

A Family Dinner

Little Dorrit

—◆—

Mr. F's Aunt is Conducted into Retirement
H.K. Browne (Phiz)

Little Dorrit opens with a surprisingly luscious feast of "sausage of Lyons, veal in savoury jelly, white bread, strachino cheese, and good wine" in a miserable jail in Marseilles; and the two themes of nourishment and imprisonment, both physical and psychological, are interwoven throughout the story.

The scenes in the Marshalsea debtor's prison are drawn straight from Dickens' childhood experience, when his father was imprisoned for debt and he, age 12, was sent to work in a blacking factory. Dickens eventually moved nearer to the Marshalsea in order to take meals with his family, as relatives were allowed into and out of the prison during the day. The pages of *Little Dorrit* reflect those early experiences of good food in bad circumstances, and family meals that aren't the happy occasions they should be.

Arthur Clennam, on his return to England, is pressed into staying for an uncomfortable family dinner with his former sweetheart Flora Finching (née Casby), now widowed, and her family. Everything is well-regulated and the dinner is "neatly served and well-cooked"—soup, fried soles, shrimp sauce, and potato are followed by mutton, steak, and an apple pie. But it is a "disenchanted feast," owing to poor Flora's embarrassing fondness for food, porter, and flirting.

Plump Flora's comfort eating contrasts with Little Dorrit's childlike body and "extraordinary repugnance to dining in company." Today we might be worried by these apparent signs of an eating disorder, but to Dickens it was "another of the moral phenomena" of Little Dorrit.

The invalid Mrs. Clennam, imprisoned in her home, dines luxuriously on partridges and oysters, but eats alone. Sharing food, particularly with those in need, has a powerful emotional pull in Dickens' works, and we soften to Flora when she takes Little Dorrit under her wing and begs her to have a good breakfast of roast fowl and ham with her tea.

LEG OF MUTTON STUFFED WITH OYSTERS

Young John Chivery, son of the Marshalsea Turnkeeper, is rewarded for running "mysterious missions" with a banquet, for which Miss Rugg "with her own hands stuffed a leg of mutton with oysters." Dickens invited Daniel Maclise to share the same dish before a night walk through the slums (letter, November 20, 1840), and later invented his own twist, adding veal to the stuffing, served at the office of his journal, *Household Words*.

SERVES 6–8

2 tablespoons freshly chopped flat-leaf parsley

1 dessertspoon freshly chopped thyme leaves

1 dessertspoon freshly chopped savory

2 hard-boiled egg yolks

6 oysters, cleaned, shucked, and chopped, reserving the liquor, or 6 finely chopped anchovies

3 garlic cloves, minced (I think garlic is better than onion in this dish, but if you prefer to follow Catherine, use one very finely chopped shallot)

leg of mutton (or lamb if you cannot find mutton), approx. 5½–6¾ lb/2.5–3kg

2 teaspoons all-purpose/plain flour

1¼ cups/300ml lamb or chicken stock

Preheat the oven to 425°F/220°C/Gas 7.

Chop the herbs as finely as possible—a meat cleaver is useful for this. Bind them together with the egg yolks, oysters (or anchovies), and garlic (or shallot).

Using a sharp knife, make about 6 indentations in the fleshy part of the leg of mutton (or lamb) and push in the mixture. If you make the indentations at a slight angle, you can pull the fat back over the cut.

Place the meat in a roasting pan and roast in the preheated oven for about 30 minutes, then turn the oven down to 325°F/160°C/Gas 3. Baste the joint with the fat and juices in the pan and continue roasting for 15–20 minutes per 1 lb/450g.

When the meat is done, remove it from the oven, cover with foil, and let it rest for 15–20 minutes.

Make the gravy by mixing the flour with the fat in the roasting dish over a low heat, and slowly adding the stock and the oyster liquor. Skim the fat off the gravy (putting it in the freezer helps it coagulate on the top) and serve as it is, or add to the Piquant Sauce ingredients (see page 24).

LEG OF MUTTON
WITH OYSTERS

Parboil some fine well-fed oysters,
take off the beards and horny parts,
put to them some parsley, minced
onions, and sweet herbs boiled and
chopped fine, and the yolks of two
or three hard-boiled eggs: mix all
together, and make five or six holes
in the fleshy part of a leg of mutton,
and put in the mixture, and dress it
in either of the following ways; tie it
up in a cloth and let it boil gently
two and a half or three hours
according to the size, or braise it,
and serve it with a pungent
brown sauce.

CATHERINE DICKENS,
What Shall We Have for Dinner?,
1851

PIQUANT SAUCE

1 shallot, finely chopped

a little oil

1 tablespoon finely chopped gherkins

1 tablespoon finely chopped capers

4 tablespoons good red wine vinegar

1 anchovy fillet, pounded

Sweat the shallot in the oil until it softens, then add the gherkins, capers, and vinegar. Simmer for 4 minutes.

Make gravy from the joint (see page 22), add the oyster liquor (to make about 1¼ cups/300ml), the shallot mixture, and the pounded anchovy. Simmer for a few minutes before serving in a gravy boat.

PIQUANT SAUCE

First prepare of gherkins, capers, and shallots, all chopped as fine as dust, a tablespoonful of each; place these in a small stewpan with a little pepper and a wineglassful of vinegar; set this to boil for about four minutes, then add rather better than half a pint of good stock, an ounce of brown thickening, no 9, a small bit of glaze and a teaspoonful of anchovy; boil, skim and pour into a small stewpan for use.

CHARLES ELME FRANCATELLI, *The Cook's Guide and Housekeeper's and Butler's Assistant*, 1861

~⌐ BAKED SOLE ⌐~

Serving this most prestigious of fish meant something. Mr. Casby shows that his household is established and well-heeled; Uncle Sol and his nephew aim to demonstrate that they are men of business in the city (*Dombey and Son*); the imposter, Jingle, is delighted to accept a dish that is served for "political dinners" (*The Pickwick Papers*). Catherine Dickens hints at the family's status through choosing sole frequently, and poor-man's food, such as mollusks like whelks or winkles, not at all.

SERVES 4

2 whole lemon or Dover sole, or 4 fillets

salt

1 egg

3½ tablespoons/50g warm but not hot butter, plus extra for greasing

a pinch of cayenne pepper

a pinch of ground mace

a pinch of ground nutmeg

1¾ cups/100g fine day-old breadcrumbs

Preheat the oven to 400°F/200°C/Gas 6. Butter a baking dish large enough to contain the fish in one layer.

Wash the fish and dry with kitchen paper. Dust both sides with a little salt.

Beat together the egg and warm butter and brush the fish all over. Place the fish skin side down in the buttered baking dish. Combine the spices with the breadcrumbs and press the mixture on top of the fish.

Bake in the preheated oven. The fillets should be ready in 8–10 minutes; whole fish in about 15–18 minutes. The fish is baked when the flesh is firm and white and flakes easily. Serve with Shrimp Sauce (see page 28).

BAKED SOLES

Fresh large soles, dressed in the following manner, are remarkably tender and delicate eating; much more so than those which are fried. After the fish has been skinned and cleansed in the usual way, wipe it dry, and let it remain for an hour or more, if time will permit, closely folded in a clean cloth; then mix with a slightly beaten egg about an ounce of butter, just liquefied but not heated at the mouth of the oven, or before the fire; brush the fish in every part with this mixture, and cover it with very fine dry bread-crumbs, seasoned with a little salt, cayenne, pounded mace, and nutmeg.

Pour a teaspoonful or two of liquid butter into a flat dish which will contain the fish well; lay it in, sprinkle it with a little more butter, press the breadcrumbs lightly on it with a broad-bladed knife, and bake it in a moderate oven for about twenty minutes. If two or more soles are required for table at the same time, they should be placed separately, quite flat, in a large dish, or each fish should be laid on a dish by itself.

On our first essay of this receipt, the fish dressed by it (it was baked for twenty-five minutes in a very slack iron oven) proved infinitely nicer than one of the same size which was fried, and served with it. The difference between them was very marked, especially as regarded the exceeding tenderness of the flesh of that which was baked; its appearance, however, would have been somewhat improved by a rather quicker oven.

When ready to serve, it should be gently glided on to the dish in which it is to be sent to table. About three ounces of bread-crumbs, and two and a half of butter, will be sufficient for a large pair of soles. They will be more perfectly encrusted with the bread if dipped into, or sprinkled with it a second time, after the first coating has been well moistened with the batter.

ELIZA ACTON, *Modern Cookery for Private Families*, 1845

SHRIMP SAUCE

Catherine frequently pairs sole with shrimp sauce. Dickens' own careful pairing in *Little Dorrit* contrasts the casual luxury of "a butter-boat of shrimp sauce" as one of many dishes in the wealthy Casby household, with shrimps as a tea-time treat at the Marshalsea. As a child, Little Dorrit is taken for outings featuring tea-gardens, and shrimps, ale, and other delicacies.

⅓ cup/75g unsalted butter

a pinch of ground mace

a pinch of cayenne pepper

juice of ½ a lemon

1 tablespoon crème fraîche

about 22 miniature shrimp/ 100g brown shrimps or two pots of potted shrimps (in which case use the butter on top of the shrimps)

1 tablespoon freshly chopped herbs (chervil, parsley, chives, and/or dill)

Heat the butter in a skillet/frying pan until it is nut brown. Add the mace, cayenne, and lemon juice. Let it bubble for a minute or two.

Whisk in the crème fraîche, then add the shrimps and warm through. Pour over and around the fish and sprinkle with freshly chopped herbs.

SHRIMP SAUCE

The fish for this sauce should be very fresh. Shell quickly one pint of shrimps and mix them with half a pint of melted butter, to which a few drops of essence of anchovies and a little mace and cayenne have been added. As soon as the shrimps are heated through, dish and serve the sauce, which ought not to boil after they are put in. Many persons add a few spoonsful of rich cream to all shell-fish sauces.

Shrimps, 1 pint; melted butter, ½ pint; essence of anchovies, 1 teaspoonful; mace, ¼ teaspoonful; cayenne, very little.

ELIZA ACTON, *Modern Cookery for Private Families*, 1845

MASHED AND BROWN POTATOES

In spite of the disastrous potato blight in the 1840s and the resulting famine in Ireland, "a dish of potatoes" was still demanded for English tables such as the Casbys. Catherine Dickens served them at nearly every meal, frequently "mashed and brown," made from what Margaret Dods admired as the Scottish and Irish "dry farinaceous" variety of potato; rather than the "cheesy, waxy roots" that she believed Londoners relished.

SERVES 4

2 lb/900g floury potatoes, peeled and quartered, eyes and discolored parts cut out

2 tablespoons milk or heavy/double cream

½ cup/100g butter, plus extra for baking

1 egg, beaten

salt

Preheat the oven to 400°F/200°C/Gas 6.

Cook the potatoes in a pan of salted boiling water until you can easily pierce them with the point of a knife. Drain well and return the pan to a low heat for a few seconds to make sure the potatoes are dry; add the milk or cream and the butter and when it has melted, mash well. It helps to do this over a very low heat, but don't let the bottom of the pan burn. Don't over-mash or they will become gluey.

Spoon or pipe the mashed potato into a gratin dish, or individual dishes or scallop shells. Brush with beaten egg and dot with butter.

Bake for 15–30 minutes (depending on the size of the dish) until the top is well browned.

MASHED AND BROWN POTATOES

Mashed Potatoes may be pressed into patty pans previously buttered, and turned out and browned; or put into stoneware scallop-shell shapes, glazed with eggs, and browned before the fire, sticking a few bits of butter upon them. A few of these make a pretty supper-dish.

MARGARET DODS, *The Cook and Housewife's Manual*, 1826

WHAT SHALL WE HAVE FOR DINNER?

In 1851 Catherine Dickens published her own bestselling book. *What Shall We Have for Dinner?* was a book of menus, or "Bills of Fare" for between 2 and 20 people, which ran to four further editions until 1860. Although there are no records of the book in the Dickenses' correspondence, their eldest son, Charley, reported (in "Reminiscences of My Father" in the Christmas 1934 supplement of *Windsor Magazine*), that the book was written by Catherine in the "Tavistock House days" and published under her pseudonym, Lady Maria Clutterbuck. Catherine had played the part of Lady Maria, the rather unattractive wife of Sir Jonas Clutterbuck, in the farce *Used Up*, which the family performed on January 15, 1851, while staying at Rockingham Castle. The pseudonym feels uncomfortably ironic, given Dickens' later repudiation of her. At the time, though, he was pleased with her housekeeping and hostessing and, as the book was published a few months after the death of her eight-month-old baby Dora (Catherine would be buried in the same grave 28 years later), it probably offered a welcome distraction from her grief.

Catherine's "bills of fare" are well-structured, and full of variety, richness, excitement, and color. Those for 14, 18, or 20 persons are dramas in five acts, featuring prestigious sole, or complicated and time-consuming jellies (made by boiling up calves' feet and flavored with Punch or Noyau, an almond-flavored liqueur). Oyster curry, veal olives, Italian cream, lamb's head and mince, and sea kale tell us something about high Victorian taste, and mutton features in almost every meal. She also offers a number of recipes for her favorite dishes, many of them taken from the popular cookery writers of the day, particularly Alexis Soyer, and the Scottish writer Christian Isobel Johnstone, who published her cookbook under the pseudonym Margaret Dods. These recipes flesh out the cursory mentions of "beef" or "fowl" or "pudding" that her husband served up in his novels.

Charles Dickens loved to eat with friends, and his notes to them are full of invitations to dine. Their household budget would be blown on glamorous food for big dinners of between 8 and 20. "Two woodcocks, hare, four snipes" or "boiled salmon, lobster sauce, filleted lobster, shrimp sauce, cucumbers" are aspirational for a middle-class household.

Literary letters of the time are abuzz with reports of "pleasant" (Longfellow) or "charming" (Mrs. Cowden-Clarke) dinners with Dickens, while Wilkie Collins

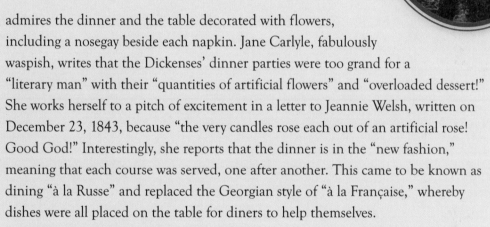

Catherine Dickens, loyal wife and author (under a pseudonym) of What Shall We Have for Dinner?

admires the dinner and the table decorated with flowers, including a nosegay beside each napkin. Jane Carlyle, fabulously waspish, writes that the Dickenses' dinner parties were too grand for a "literary man" with their "quantities of artificial flowers" and "overloaded dessert!" She works herself to a pitch of excitement in a letter to Jeannie Welsh, written on December 23, 1843, because "the very candles rose each out of an artificial rose! Good God!" Interestingly, she reports that the dinner is in the "new fashion," meaning that each course was served, one after another. This came to be known as dining "à la Russe" and replaced the Georgian style of "à la Française," whereby dishes were all placed on the table for diners to help themselves.

Catherine's low-cost suggestions for family dinners of suet dumplings, minced beef with bacon, turnip tops, and endless "mashed and brown potatoes" helped to balance the domestic books. Her Edinburgh upbringing was relatively humble; her parents couldn't afford to keep a cook, so she learned domestic economy and Scottish dishes, such as cock-a-leekie soup and Scotch mutton broth, from her mother. Her menus are practical, reflecting what a middle-class housekeeper with limited oven and stove-top space in an urban kitchen could produce. It is not diet food, though, and Catherine, unsurprisingly for a Victorian mother of 10, became plump. It was one of the complaints Dickens made about her on their separation, and his unflattering reports of her incompetence and mental instability prevailed with biographers for many years. However, recent scholarship on the couple's letters, Catherine's life, and *What Shall We Have for Dinner?* shows her to have been kind, competent, and resourceful.

APPLE PUDDING

Henry Dickens recalled a joke his mother liked to tell about a Scotswoman's
view of Eve being tempted in Paradise: "Eh mon, it would be nae temptation
to me to gae rinning aboot a gairden stairk naked 'ating green apples."
Catherine gives recipes for Eve's pudding and also this light apple pudding,
which she must have encountered in Switzerland, known as a Betty
or Charlotte in England.

SERVES 6

2 lb 3 oz/1kg cooking apples

½ cup/100g soft brown sugar
(or to taste), plus an extra
dessertspoon

2 tablespoons/30g butter

3 cups/175g day-old
breadcrumbs

½ teaspoon ground nutmeg

Preheat the oven to 375°F/190°C/Gas 5.

Peel, core, and slice the cooking apples. Place in a saucepan with the
sugar and 1 tablespoon water, cover, and cook for 5–10 minutes
until soft.

Melt the butter in a large skillet/frying pan and fry the breadcrumbs
until they are lightly golden brown. Sprinkle in the nutmeg.

Put half the breadcrumbs in the bottom of an ovenproof dish
(approx. 2¾–3½ pints/1.5–2 litres), pushing them down in the
center so they rise up slightly at the sides. Add the stewed apple and
put the remaining breadcrumbs on top. Sprinkle the top with the
extra sugar.

Warm through in the preheated oven for 15–20 minutes.

SWISS PUDDING

*Butter your dish, lay in it a layer of bread crumbs grated very fine, then boil four or five apples
very tender, add a little butter, nutmeg, and fine sifted sugar, mix all up together and lay on the
bread crumbs, then another layer of the crumbs, then add pieces of fresh butter on the top, and
bake in a slow oven for a quarter of an hour, until it become a delicate brown.*

CATHERINE DICKENS, *What Shall We Have for Dinner?*, 1851

CHEESE SOUFFLE

Cheese—usually grilled or toasted—is a favorite savory in Catherine Dickens' book. Her eldest son, Charley, reminiscing on their dinners, wondered, "how many dinners were begun with a glass of Chichester milk-punch; how many were finished with a dish of toasted cheese?" This simple recipe, taken from Alexis Soyer, is an easy-to-make soufflé without the white sauce preparation.

SERVES 4

⅔ cup/50g grated Parmesan

3½ tablespoons/50g butter, softened, plus extra for greasing

1½ cups/130g grated Cheddar or Gruyère, or other strong full-fat cheese

3½ tablespoons/50ml heavy/double cream or sour cream

6 US extra-large/ UK large eggs, separated

a pinch of cream of tartar

a pinch each of sea salt, finely ground black pepper, and cayenne

Optional flavorings

½ teaspoon Dijon mustard

2 teaspoons finely chopped herbs, such as chives, thyme, or tarragon

Preheat the oven to 350°F/180°C/Mark 4. Grease a 3½-pint/2-litre soufflé or baking dish. Tip the grated Parmesan into the dish and roll it around to coat the sides evenly. Tip any remaining Parmesan out of the dish and add to the rest of the cheese.

Put the softened butter, cheese, cream, egg yolks, seasonings, and mustard, if using, into a bowl and blend or whisk with an electric blender until very well combined. Add the chopped herbs, if using.

Put the egg whites and cream of tartar into a clean bowl and whisk until stiff. Fold the whisked egg whites into the cheese mixture, a little at a time, and then pour into the prepared soufflé dish.

Bake in the preheated oven for about 30–35 minutes until it is puffed up and golden brown. Eat immediately, accompanied by Watercress Salad (see page 51).

FONDUE (SIMPLE METHOD)

Put two ounces of Gruyère and two ounces of Parmesan cheese (grated) into a basin (or if you have not got them use English cheese), with a little salt, pepper, and cayenne, add the yolks of six eggs with a quarter of a pound of butter melted (mix well), whip the whites of the six eggs, stir gently into the other ingredients, fill small paper cases (or one large paper case) with it, bake about a quarter of an hour in a moderate oven, and serve very hot.

CATHERINE DICKENS, *What Shall We Have for Dinner?*, 1851

CHAPTER 3

Bella's Food for Loved Ones

Our Mutual Friend

———◆———

The Wedding Dinner at Greenwich
Marcus Stone

In spite of Dickens' reputation as a writer of conviviality, in his stories food specifically designed to mark a public expression of affection usually does anything but. Miss Havisham's cobwebby wedding cake in *Great Expectations*, the "splendid cake, covered with Cupids, silver, and true-lovers' knots" set out for the mutually deceiving Lammles in *Our Mutual Friend*, the Dombeys' chilly wedding breakfast —all are mockeries of wedded happiness.

The two nuptial meals shared by Bella Wilfer, John Rokesmith, and Cherubic Pa in *Our Mutual Friend* stand out for their success. In Dickens' moral world, enjoying a simple meal of bread and butter is often a sign of integrity, so the little tea of milk and a cottage loaf at Pa's workplace to celebrate Bella and John's impromptu betrothal is a good omen for their happiness.

The happiest meals are usually the most intimate. Bella and John take their wedding breakfast with Pa (Ma having been excluded from both the ceremony and the feast) in the Thames estuary suburb of Greenwich. Greenwich drew daytrippers and political parties alike—and Dickens himself invited friends on several occasions—to taverns for its famous Whitebait Dinners. Their own dinner of "specimens of all the fishes that swim in the sea," in celebrating their "partnership of three," contrasts with the usual crowds.

In the same book, the Veneerings' aspirational dinners are marked by perfect correctness of form and tableware, but Dickens gives no hint about the food—the impression is of parties with no flavor, warmth, or nourishment, reflecting the insincerity and dishonesty of the hosts.

The image of a young woman cooking for somebody out of love enchanted Dickens with its emotional appeal and comic potential. Bella, trying to cook a meal to celebrate her parents' wedding anniversary, twirls the spit so often that the fowls end up underdone but Pa puts it right with the gridiron, with Bella's help, and it is this father-daughter relationship, rather than the perfect meal, that makes him happy.

GREENWICH WHITEBAIT

The taverns of Greenwich and Blackwall in south-east London became famous for their summer dinners of whitebait, and the Dickenses entertained friends at inns including the Crown and Sceptre, the Trafalgar, and the Ship. When Bella and John, and Bella's beloved Pa, enjoy their whitebait wedding feast, Dickens writes that the dishes were "seasoned with Bliss—an article which they are sometimes out of, at Greenwich."

SERVES 4

1 lb 9 oz/700g whitebait

4–5 tablespoons all-purpose/plain flour, seasoned well with salt and freshly ground black pepper

vegetable oil, for frying

lemon wedges, to serve

For devilled whitebait

½ teaspoon each of mustard powder and cayenne pepper, plus a pinch of paprika

Wash the whitebait and drain on kitchen paper.

When completely dry, toss them in the seasoned flour. (It may be easiest to do this by putting the flour and seasoning in a plastic bag, tossing the fish in, then tipping them into a strainer/sieve to get rid of the excess flour.) If making devilled whitebait, add the extra seasonings to the flour too.

Heat the oil in a deep-fat fryer or a high-sided pan half-full of oil to about 375°F/190°C (this is when a cube of bread browns in about 20 seconds).

Fry the whitebait in batches for 3 minutes at a time. If there are too many fish in the fryer/pan at once, they will reduce the temperature of the oil and become greasy instead of crisp and golden.

Remove with a wire or slotted spoon and tip onto folded kitchen paper to drain off excess oil. Eat while still very hot, with lemon wedges to squeeze over and bread and butter on the side.

TO DRESS WHITE BAIT (GREENWICH RECEIPT)

(In season in July, August, and September). This delicate little fish requires great care to dress it well. Do not touch it with the hands, but throw it from your dish or basket into a cloth, with three or four handsful of flour, and shake it well; then put it into a bait sieve, to separate it from the superfluous flour. Have ready a very deep frying-pan, nearly full of boiling fat, throw in the fish, which will be done in an instant; they must not be allowed to take any colour, for if browned, they are spoiled. Lift them out, and dish them upon a silver or earthenware drainer, without a napkin, piling them very high in the centre. Send them to table with a cut lemon, and slices of brown bread and butter.

ELIZA ACTON, *Modern Cookery for Private Families*, 1845

COD WITH OYSTER SAUCE

Dickens alluded to the oyster's reputation as an aphrodisiac in the title of an early sketch, *Love and Oysters* (later renamed *The Misplaced Attachment of Mr. John Dounce* for publication in *Sketches by Boz*). When Catherine was nine months pregnant, he wrote ruefully to his oyster-loving American friend, Felton, "total abstinence from oysters seems to be the best thing for me" (January 2, 1844). The oyster sauce with cod that features frequently on Catherine's menus is reproduced here by combining two of Mrs. Marshall's elegant recipes.

SERVES 4

For the sauce

8–12 oysters

2¼ cups/500ml fish stock

¾ cup/200ml dry white wine

1 teaspoon tarragon vinegar or mild white wine vinegar

6 black peppercorns

2 bay leaves

Julienne Vegetables (see page 42) (optional)

⅔ cup/150ml light/single cream

a pinch of cayenne pepper

freshly chopped flat-leaf parsley, to garnish

For the cod

approx. 1 lb 10 oz/750g cod, cut into four fillets

salt

softened butter, for greasing

To serve

1 lemon cut into quarters

Open the oysters into a sieve over a bowl, reserving the liquor.

Put the fish stock, wine, vinegar, peppercorns, and bay leaves into a wide saucepan and bring to a rolling boil. Add the julienne vegetables (if using) and let them simmer for a few minutes until just cooked, then remove and keep warm. Continue to cook the stock until it is reduced by half, then discard the bay leaves and peppercorns.

Sprinkle salt onto the cod and brush the skin with soft butter, to stop it sticking in the pan.

Stir the oyster liquor into the rest of the liquid in the pan. Lay the cod fillets in the pan in one layer, skin side down, then put the lid on the pan and steam for 4–5 minutes.

Carefully remove the fish, place it on top of the vegetables, and keep warm.

Add the cream to the poaching liquor and heat it through, reducing the liquor until it is the desired consistency. Add a pinch of cayenne, taste for seasoning, and add a pinch of salt if you need it. Add the oysters to the sauce to warm through.

Put the oysters on top of the fish and spoon over the sauce. Sprinkle with the chopped parsley and serve with the lemon quarters.

OYSTER SAUCE

Blanch half a dozen large or twelve small oysters in their own liquor, strain them, remove the beards, and cut each oyster, if large, into two or three pieces. Put four tablespoonfuls of French vinegar into a stewpan with six or eight peppercorns and two bayleaves, reduce till the vinegar is half the quantity, then add four raw yolks of eggs and half a gill of oyster liquor and work in by degrees two ounces of butter, standing the pan in the bain marie while doing so, season with a tiny dust of cayenne or white pepper and a pinch of salt, strain the sauce through the tammy, warm it up again in the bain marie, add the oysters and serve in a hot sauceboat.

COD A LA GRAND HOTEL
(Cabillaud à la Grand Hotel)

Cleanse the cod and cut it in slices about two inches thick, and sprinkle these well with salt. Let them stay in the salt for about an hour, then wash them well in cold water and tie them up with tape. Put about two ounces of butter, the juice of a lemon, and about two and a half wineglasses of white wine (this is for three to four pounds of fish) in the bottom of a stewpan, lay the cod slices in this, with a buttered paper over them, and let it all simmer at the side of the stove for fifteen to twenty minutes, then take the fish up with a slice and place it on a hot dish, pour the sauce round it, with some more served in a sauceboat, and garnish the fillets all round the edge with salsify or parsnip cut in Julienne shreds, and sprigs of picked and blanched chervil. Sprinkle the centre of the fish with a little lobster coral. Serve very hot.

MRS. A.B. MARSHALL'S *Cookery Book*, 1888

JULIENNE VEGETABLES

With the cod (see page 39), Mrs. Marshall suggests serving salsify—also known as the oyster plant because of its oystery taste when cooked. It is hard to find nowadays. Sea kale, which Catherine also includes in her menus, would be an excellent vegetable to go with fish; but it was gathered almost to extinction by Victorians, so use samphire instead for that salty, seaside taste. Other vegetables that julienne well are carrots, celery, and zucchini/courgettes.

Cut the vegetables into neat batons about 2 inches/5cm long.

Cook briefly in boiling water or, if serving with the cod with oyster sauce on page 39, you could throw them into the stock and white wine to cook as it reduces. Lift them out of the pan and plate them, keeping them warm while you cook the cod; then place a piece of fish on top of each, and pour the sauce over.

JULIENNE GARNISH

Peel and cut the vegetables such as carrots, turnips, &c into strips about an inch long, blanch each separately by putting them in pans with sufficient cold water to cover them, and bringing them to the boil, then straining them; put them back in the separate pans with boiling water and a little salt, and cook them till tender, then strain them, pour a little warm butter over each and use.

MRS. A.B. MARSHALL'S *Cookery Book*, 1888

RUTH PINCH'S BEEFSTEAK PUDDING

In *Martin Chuzzlewit*, Ruth Pinch—the sort of ingénue housekeeper that Dickens loved writing about—is worried that the beefsteak pudding she cooks for her brother Tom will "turn out a stew, or a soup, or something of that sort." Tom enjoys watching her cook, but later teases her when they realize she should have used suet for the pastry. Eliza Acton gives Ruth the last word by devising "Ruth Pinch's Beefsteak Pudding," made with butter and eggs.

SERVES 4

For the pastry

3½ cups/450g self-rising flour

a pinch of salt

⅔ cup/150g cold butter, cubed, plus extra for greasing

3 eggs

For the filling

1 lb 2 oz/500g stewing steak, cubed

1 onion, finely chopped

2 teaspoons freshly chopped thyme

2 teaspoons freshly chopped parsley

3 level tablespoons all-purpose/plain flour

about ⅔ cup/150ml beef stock (or water plus a tablespoon of Worcestershire sauce or mushroom ketchup)

salt and freshly ground black pepper

And any of Eliza Acton's suggested additions:

a few whole oysters

or 5½ oz/150g kidney, chopped (Eliza recommended "veal kidneys seasoned with fine herbs")

or 6 oz/170g "nicely prepared button mushrooms"

or a few shavings of fresh truffle

or 5–7 oz/150–200g sweetbreads, chopped

Start by making the pastry. Sieve the flour and salt into a basin; add the butter and rub it in. Beat the eggs together with a dash of cold water, then stir them into the flour mixture with a wooden spoon.

Pull the mixture together with your hands, adding a little more water or flour as necessary. When you have an elastic dough, turn it onto a lightly floured board and roll out into a large disc. Cut a quarter out and put to one side.

Fold the two outer quarters over the middle quarter and put into a well-buttered 2-pint/1.2-litre basin, with the point in the bottom. Unfold the two outer quarters and push the pastry into the sides of the basin, wetting the edges so that they seal together and the whole basin is fully lined. Trim the top edge so there is ½–1 inch/1–2cm of pastry overhanging the edge of the basin.

Roll out the remaining quarter to make a circular lid.

Mix the meat with the remaining ingredients except the liquid, making sure the flour is well distributed. Turn it into the pastry-lined basin and pour the

stock or liquid over. Brush the top edge of the pastry in the basin with water and put the pastry lid on top, pinching it around to seal.

Put a lid of buttered foil or a circle of parchment or greaseproof paper and a cloth on top, adding a pleat to give room for the pudding to puff up.

Place the basin in a saucepan so that the water comes halfway up the side of the pudding. Cover and steam for up to 4 hours, checking and topping up the water level every half hour or so.

Serve straight from the bowl or turn it out and cut it into segments. The butter crust makes this easier to do than the traditional suet one.

SMALL BEEF-STEAK PUDDING

Make into a very firm smooth paste, one pound of flour, six ounces of beef suet finely minced, half a teaspoonful of salt, and half a pint of cold water. Line with this a basin which holds a pint and a half. Season a pound of tender steak, free from bone and skin, with half an ounce of salt and half a teaspoonful of pepper well mixed together; lay it in the crust, pour in a quarter of a pint of water, roll out the cover, close the pudding carefully, tie a floured cloth over, and boil it for three hours and a half. We give this receipt in addition to the preceding one, as an exact guide for the proportions of meat-puddings in general.

Flour, 1lb; suet, 6oz; salt, ½ teaspoonful; water, ½ pint; rump steak, 1lb; salt, ½oz; pepper, ½ teaspoonful; water, ¼ pint: 3½ hours.

RUTH PINCH'S BEEF-STEAK PUDDING

To make Ruth Pinch's celebrated pudding (known also as beef-steak pudding à la Dickens) substitute six ounces of butter for the suet in this receipt, and moisten the paste with the well-beaten yolk of four eggs, or with three whole ones, mixed with a little water; butter the basin very thickly before the paste is laid in, as the pudding is to be turned out of it for table. In all else proceed exactly as above.

ELIZA ACTON, *Modern Cookery for Private Families*, 1845

HOUSEKEEPING AND THE KITCHEN

Every generation tends to believe that their young women are far more inept in the kitchen than their mothers. Victorians had more justification than some, as industrialization attracted many young women to cities for employment, away from their mothers and grandmothers and the lessons they could learn from them. Harriet Martineau, writing in Dickens' journal, *Household Words*, called for a "New School for Wives" for factory women, to include "the most important of the domestic arts of life—and first, Cookery" (April 10, 1852).

A publishing industry ballooned to capitalize on the market of middle-class young women, uncertain of their knowledge of cookery, housekeeping, and etiquette. The most successful was Samuel Beeton's *The Englishwoman's Domestic Magazine*, the domestic supplements of which were published as *Mrs. Beeton's Book of Household Management* in 1861. Poor women had to get by without the luxury of instruction or kitchen implements and, like Mrs. Cratchit, certainly no oven. Cast-iron ovens were beginning to replace brick ovens in the wealthiest houses at the beginning of the nineteenth century. Experienced cooks threw sawdust into an oven and gauged its heat by how quickly it turned brown. Mr. Pickwick's landlady, Mrs. Bardell, who has a "natural genius for cooking," has cheese simmering away for her girlfriends' supper in the thick, tightly lidded casserole known as a Dutch Oven. Bella Wilfer does battle with an old-fashioned spit, but a more modern gadget in Victorian times was the roasting jack, driven by clockwork. Both, used properly, allowed the meat fibers to cook and relax alternately, giving a delicious result.

Dickens and his readers were charmed by the image of the ingénue housekeeper, whose inexperience and mistakes were captivating, so long as they were accompanied by willingness to learn. Esther Summerson, although "quite lost in the magnitude of my trust" when she is given the housekeeper's keys to Bleak House, believes they sound like "little bells" that ring her "hopefully to bed" and make housekeeping her joyful duty. Bella Wilfer and Ruth Pinch's attempts to cook for those they love have something pure and wholehearted about them, and their happy endings are assured. Life with David Copperfield's Dora, though, is "not comfortable"; she plays with her dog, Jip, instead of consulting the cookbook or doing the household accounts, and is incapable of producing a properly cooked meal, so she is obliged to die and give her place to the capable and virtuous Agnes.

Bella's Food for Loved Ones

An early Victorian kitchen, showing a bottle jack being used to roast a joint of meat before the fire.

Poor Dora had Peggotty to live up to; she, along with *Bleak House*'s Mrs. Bagnet, is one of the few mature women in the novels who is loving and competent—indeed, a taste of her "apple parsties" inspires the carter, Barkis, to declare his willingness to marry her. Dickens, perhaps remembering his own mother, who wanted him to go out to work rather than school, generally draws unflattering portraits of flawed housekeepers such as Pip's frightening sister in *Great Expectations* or the hysterical Mrs. Bardell, who sues Mr. Pickwick. *Bleak House*'s Mrs. Jellaby is the most exquisitely bad housekeeper of them all, busy writing letters on behalf of the "natives of Borrioboola-Gha" while her half-fed and half-clothed children tumble down the stairs.

Dickens was unusual among middle-class Victorian men for knowing his way around the kitchen, and he is happy to include men in its moral sphere. Captain Cuttle, making Florence Dombey a hot meal of chicken, sausage, potato, gravy, and egg sauce, shows more virtue and usefulness than her wealthy, chilly father had ever done. The self-indulgent Eugene Wrayburn in *Our Mutual Friend* kits out his kitchen with the latest gadgets, including a miniature flour barrel, coffee mill, and roasting jack, in the hope that these domestic objects will make him virtuous, and, in Dickens' moral universe, his desire for domestic goodness is what saves his life.

ROAST FOWL

There are innumerable roast fowl in Dickens: the working Gargerys in *Great Expectations* have a pair for Christmas dinner, and Flora Casby tries to entice Little Dorrit with a leg of fowl for breakfast. Bella Wilfer in *Our Mutual Friend* insists on cooking them for her parents' anniversary dinner, twirling them on the spit so fast that they are pink inside; "is it the breed?" she asks Cherubic Pa. Alexis Soyer's lovely recipe is here adapted to pot-roasting, which suits modern-day chickens better than boiling.

SERVES 4

2¾–3¼ lb/1.25–1.5kg free-range chicken

½ a lemon

a few sprigs of tarragon, plus 30–40 leaves

2 slices of unsmoked streaky bacon

oil, for frying

2 onions, thickly sliced

2 or 3 carrots, thickly sliced

1 or 2 turnips, thickly sliced

2 sticks of celery

2 bay leaves

a few sprigs of thyme

a wineglass of sherry or 2–3 glasses of white wine, plus enough stock to make about 2¼ cups/500ml liquid

salt, freshly ground black pepper, and nutmeg, to season

Preheat the oven to 350°F/180°C/Gas 4.

Rub the skin of the chicken all over with the half lemon, then put the lemon in the bird's cavity with the sprigs of tarragon. Season the chicken inside and out with a little salt, pepper, and nutmeg.

Chop the bacon and fry quickly in a very little oil in the bottom of a large casserole. Add the onions and fry until they are beginning to soften.

Add the remaining vegetables, turn them in the oil, and let them sweat for a minute or two. Add the bay leaves, thyme, and sherry or wine, and bring to the boil; bubble for a moment, then add the stock and bring back to the boil, then turn off the heat.

Place the chicken on top of the vegetables. Put a lid on and put in the oven. Cook for 1 hour with the lid on, then remove it and cook for another 30–45 minutes, to brown the chicken skin.

When it is cooked through and the juices run clear, take the chicken out of the casserole and keep warm.

Strain the cooking juices into a small pan and reduce to thicken. Add the tarragon leaves and serve the gravy separately.

CAPON OR POULARD A L'ESTRAGON

I have been told many fanciful epicures idolize this dish. The bird should be trussed for boiling. Rub the breast with half a lemon, tie over it some thin slices of bacon, cover the bottom of a small stewpan with thin slices of the same, and a few trimmings of either beef, veal, or lamb, two onions, a little carrot, turnip and celery, two bay-leaves, one sprig of thyme, a glass of sherry, two quarts of water, season lightly with salt, pepper, and nutmeg, simmer about one hour and a quarter, keeping continually a little fire on the lid, strain three parts of the gravy into a small basin, skim off the fat, and pass through a tammy into a small stewpan, add a drop of gravy or colouring to give it a nice brown colour, boil a few minutes longer, and put about forty tarragon leaves; wash, and put it in the boiling gravy, with a tablespoonful of good French vinegar, and pour over the capon when you serve it; it is an improvement to clarify the gravy. All kinds of fowls and chickens are continually cooked in this manner in France. They are also served with rice.

ALEXIS SOYER, *The Modern Housewife or Ménagère*, 1849

WATERCRESS SALAD

Watercress selling became a little industry thanks to the Victorian innovation of year-round cultivation. The campaigning journalist Henry Mayhew interviewed an eight-year-old watercress girl, tired beyond her years, whose day began at four or five in the morning, buying "creases" to sell on for "four bunches a penny." Catherine serves it often, particularly with grilled cheese at the end of the meal (see page 35). Eliza Acton gives us the French trick of offsetting its pungency with a delicate aniseed flavor.

SERVES 1

a good handful of watercress

1 dessertspoon finely chopped tarragon

1 dessertspoon coarsely chopped chervil, if you can find it, otherwise use flat-leaf parsley

a little finely chopped scallion/spring onion (optional)

salt and freshly ground black pepper

a little light olive oil and very good white wine vinegar, to dress the leaves

Mix the leaves, herbs, and scallion/spring onion, if using, together.

Sprinkle with salt and pepper, drizzle over a little oil and vinegar, then toss to make sure each leaf is lightly dressed.

WATERCRESS SALAD FOR GARNISH

Have the leaves well washed and picked and kept in water till wanted, then dry by shaking in a clean cloth, and season them with salad oil, a little chopped tarragon and chervil, a little eschalot chopped fine, and a little salt and mignonette pepper.

ELIZA ACTON, *Modern Cookery for Private Families*, 1845

TRUE LOVERS' KNOTS

In *Our Mutual Friend*, Bella Wilfer, resisting the loveless marriage that Old
Mr. Harmon's will imposes on her, expostulates, "Talk of orange flowers
indeed!" referring to the classic association of orange blossom and brides.
When she marries for love, a young waiter puts a piece of orange blossom
by her hand. The orange-flower water is a Victorian addition to these
old-fashioned knots, the shapes of which adorn the splendid cake at
Mr. and Mrs. Lammle's society wedding.

MAKES 8–12

5 tablespoons/70g unsalted
butter, cubed

3 cups minus 2 tablespoons/
385g all-purpose/plain flour,
sifted

a pinch of salt

¾ cup/150g soft brown sugar

3 free-range eggs

zest of ½ a lemon

zest of 1 orange

2 teaspoons orange flower water

confectioner's/icing sugar, for
dusting

Preheat the oven to 325°F/170°C/Gas 3. Line two baking trays with
baking parchment paper.

Rub the butter into the flour and salt until the mixture resembles
very fine breadcrumbs, then stir in the brown sugar.

Beat the eggs, zests, and flower water together, then stir into the
flour, bringing it together to form a stiff paste. Knead it on a
well-floured surface until it is flexible.

To make lovers' knots: roll two pieces of dough into rope shapes
about 12 inches/30cm long and ½ inch/1cm in diameter. Make
a simple knot with one piece, then another simple knot with the
second piece, interlinking them to form a lovers' knot.

To make simple knots: roll ropes about 9½ inches/24cm long
and about ¾ inch/2cm wide. Tie the ends into a knot, then cut
the bottom end off and tuck the top end in to make a neat
circular shape.

Using a flat spatula or fish slice, carefully transfer the knots to the
lined baking trays. Bake in the preheated oven for 20–25 minutes
until pale gold. Cool on a wire rack and dust with sieved
confectioner's/icing sugar.

TRUE-LOVERS' KNOTS

Break six eggs into a basin, beat in 1 table-spoonful of orange-flower water, 6oz. of crushed loaf sugar, and sufficient flour to form a stiff paste. Roll this out twice and knead it well, cut off small pieces of it, roll them out long and thin, tie them into true lovers' knots, put them on a baking-sheet, and bake them a light brown in a moderate oven. In the meantime clarify 6oz. of sugar, boil it, put in the cakes, toss them in the pan over the fire until they and the sugar are quite dry and white, put them out to cool, and serve as required.

THEODORE GARRETT, *The Encyclopaedia of Practical Cookery*, Volume 1, 1892-94

CHAPTER 4

Guppy's Dining House Treat

Bleak House

— ◆ —

Mr. Guppy's Entertainment
H.K. Browne (Phiz)

Dickens' workers and travelers eat in pubs, inns, cookshops, and pie shops, and from street vendors, but the best meals out are those had for the fun of it. *The Pickwick Papers* is full of taverns and treats; and *Bleak House* has the young clerk, Mr. Guppy, entertaining his friends Mr. Smallweed (not yet 15) and the former law-writer, Mr. Jobling. Their dining house is fine enough to have a menu, so they enjoy the luxury of choice. They joke that the ravenous Mr. Jobling, who has fallen on hard times since being sacked, starts off "just born" and slowly becomes a man as he demolishes "half-and-half" (ale), veal and ham, French beans, summer cabbage, and marrow pudding until, at the stage of small rums and Cheshire cheese, "I am grown up now, Guppy. I have arrived at maturity."

The young David Copperfield eats out through necessity, being swindled along the way by an entertaining run of waiters and publicans. There is a mournfulness to these scenes of a child treating himself, alone but in public. In contrast, in *The Old Curiosity Shop*, the young Kit stakes a claim on adulthood and gentility when he takes his family to a private box in an oyster shop with his first wages. Inns might represent good food and conviviality, but patrons generally had no choice in either. In the same book, the exhausted Little Nell and her grandfather are revived on a rainy night by a blazing fire and a cauldron of stew whose ingredients, ranging from tripe to sparrow-grass (asparagus), are as ill-assorted as the traveling circus company around them.

Eating together is the thing, but there are glorious exceptions—Mrs. Gamp, in *Martin Chuzzlewit*, settles in to nurse her patient at The Bull Inn in London's Holborn, by ordering up her favorite delicacies of pickled salmon, a "cowcumber" (cucumber), and Brighton Old Tipper Ale to lighten her solitude.

CAULIFLOWER WITH PARMESAN

Although Smallweed and co. eschew the "artificially whitened cauliflowers" in favor of summer cabbage (without slugs) in *Bleak House*, Catherine's light version of cauliflower cheese makes a sophisticated side vegetable with hollandaise, rather than the usual gloopy white sauce. She probably enjoyed it on the family's sojourns in France, Italy, or Switzerland.

SERVES 6–8 AS A SIDE DISH

1 large cauliflower

7 tablespoons/100g unsalted butter

2 US extra-large/ UK large fresh, free-range egg yolks

1 tablespoon lemon juice

salt and freshly ground white pepper

a pinch of nutmeg

⅔ cup/50g grated Parmesan

Preheat the oven to 375°F/190°C/Gas 5.

Cut the cauliflower into florets (keeping the stems on) and boil or steam them until just tender. Drain and reassemble them into their cauliflower shape in a deep dish or bowl.

To make the sauce, melt the butter in a small pan. Put the egg yolks in a heatproof bowl over a pan of simmering water and whisk in the lemon juice. Whisk in the melted butter a very little at a time, keeping the whisking going all the time so the sauce does not separate (you may like to use a blender). The yolks will thicken as they cook, giving you a pouring consistency. Season with salt, white pepper, and a tiny rasp of nutmeg.

Pour the sauce over the reassembled cauliflower and sprinkle the Parmesan on the top. (The hollandaise is so rich that I've suggested using very little Parmesan, although Catherine's was a cheese-loving family and it sounds as if she used more.)

Bake in the preheated oven for 20 minutes.

TO BOIL CAULIFLOWER WITH PARMESAN

Boil a cauliflower, drain it on a sieve, and cut it into convenient-sized pieces, arrange these pieces in a pudding-basin so as to make them resemble a cauliflower on the dish, season it as you proceed, turn it on the dish, then cover it with a sauce made of grated parmesan cheese, butter, and the yolks of a couple of eggs seasoned with lemon juice, pepper, salt, and nutmeg, and put parmesan grated over it; bake for twenty minutes and brown it.

CATHERINE DICKENS, *What Shall We Have for Dinner?*, 1851

VEAL ROLLS

In *Bleak House*, Guppy, Jobling, and Smallweed order "veal and ham and French beans" for their tavern dinner, instructing the waitress not to forget the stuffing. Veal was never very popular in England; Mrs. Beeton abhorred the "inhuman and disgraceful" treatment of veal calves. Most veal recipes were adapted from French or Italian, but veal rolls or "olives" were a peculiarly British addition, particularly stuffed with good, fatty ham or bacon to prevent the veal drying out.

SERVES 4

4 slices of high-welfare veal

1 teaspoon lemon juice

1 cup/150g ham, very finely chopped

4 sage leaves, very finely chopped

1 tablespoon finely chopped flat-leaf parsley

4 scallions/spring onions, white part only, finely chopped

6 teaspoons/30g butter

1 leek (optional)

1 glass of white wine

salt and freshly ground black pepper

Place the veal slices between plastic wrap/clingfilm or wax/greaseproof paper and flatten with the back of a knife until they are $\frac{1}{8}$ inch/3-4mm thick. Season them with a little lemon juice, black pepper, and a little salt (unless your ham is salty, in which case omit it).

Mix together the finely chopped ham, herbs, scallions/spring onions, and 4 teaspoons/20g of the butter and spread this over the veal slices. Roll up the veal slices and tie them with string or a long, thin piece of leek, or skewer them with toothpicks/cocktail sticks.

Melt the remaining butter in a large ovenproof casserole, add the veal rolls, and fry them over a very gentle heat (not too high or the meat will become dry) on all sides until golden—this should only take 4-5 minutes.

Pour the wine into the casserole and let it bubble around the rolls, stirring to pick up the butter and bits from the bottom of the casserole. Cover and leave them to braise on the lowest possible heat for about 8-10 minutes.

If you need to reduce the wine, remove the veal rolls to warmed serving plates first. Serve with French beans.

VEAL ROLLS *for a side-dish, or supper-dish, may be made of long thin slices of veal flattened, seasoned, and rolled round a forcemeat of bacon or grated ham, suet, eschalot, parsley and spices. Tie the rolls tight, and stew them slowly in gravy, adding a glass of white wine and the squeeze of a lemon. Serve in a ragout-dish. Stewed mushrooms are a suitable accompaniment to this dish, which is just another name for veal-olives.*

MARGARET DODS, *The Cook and Housewife's Manual*, 1826

OXTAIL STEW

In *The Old Curiosity Shop*, Nell, her grandfather, and their eccentric fellow-travelers are revived at The Jolly Sandboys with an equally eccentric "stew of tripe… cow-heel… steak… peas, cauliflowers, new potatoes, and sparrow-grass [asparagus] all working up together in one delicious gravy." Margaret Dods' dish of oxtail rather than cow-heel, served with peas and root vegetables, is also good for a hungry crowd on a rainy night.

SERVES 4

1 oxtail, about 3¼ lb/1.5kg, cut into short lengths (your butcher will do this for you)

4 slices of unsmoked streaky bacon, chopped

olive oil, for frying

2 onions, peeled and roughly chopped

2 garlic cloves, crushed

3 carrots, peeled and roughly chopped

1 small turnip, peeled and roughly chopped

a sprig of thyme, a few stalks of parsley, and a bay leaf, tied in a bouquet or in a muslin

1 quart/1 litre organic beef stock

salt and freshly ground black pepper

sauce hachée (see right) or horseradish sauce, to serve

For the sauce hachée

2–3 gherkins, finely chopped

1 tablespoon flat-leaf parsley, leaves only, finely chopped

salt and freshly ground black pepper

Optional extra flavorings for sauce

2 scallions/spring onions, very finely chopped

or ½ teaspoon grated horseradish

or a little lemon zest

Rinse the oxtail pieces and then leave to soak in salted cold water for an hour or two.

Drain the oxtail, place in a pan of fresh water and bring to a rolling boil for 10–15 minutes, skimming the scum from the surface (this removes the bitterness).

If you are cooking the stew in the oven, preheat it to 300°F/150°C/Gas 2.

Fry the bacon in a very little olive oil in a large flameproof pot. Add the onions and garlic and sweat until they begin to soften, then add the rest of the vegetables.

Add the drained oxtail pieces to the pot, fry them a little in the fat until they start to color, then add the herbs, the beef stock, and enough water to make sure the meat is completely covered. Bring to a simmer, check the seasoning, and add a little salt if necessary. Cover and either keep on a very

low heat or put in the oven for 4 hours. Add a little water if the oxtail is becoming dry.

When the meat is falling off the bone, take the stew off the heat or remove from the oven. If the gravy is too thin, remove the meat and vegetables with a slotted spoon and boil it fast to reduce it until it is the depth of intensity you like, then add salt and pepper to taste and return the meat and vegetables.

Serve with peas, mashed carrots, and parsnips.

For the sauce hachée, simply mix the ingredients and any extra flavoring you select together and serve separately, along with a bowl of horseradish sauce. Or make horseradish mash by infusing warm milk with grated horseradish root while the potatoes are cooking.

HOTCH-POTCH OF OX-TAILS, OR RUMPS A LA MODE, A FRENCH DISH

Have the tails jointed, and blanch as for soup. Cover a stew-pan with trimmings of meat or poultry, and put in the tails, with plenty of onions, two carrots, a faggot of herbs, a bay-leaf, three cloves, and a bit of garlic. Moisten this with two ladlesful of broth, cover it with slices of bacon, then paper, then the lid, and over all a few cinders. Let it simmer for four hours, till the meat part from the bones with a spoon. Serve with a ragout of roots stewed (after boiling) in the sauce of the tails or in melted butter. Two tails will be required for a good dish. – Obs. Ox-tail dressed as above is very good served with a sauce, ie purée of the pulp of pease, or with sauce hachée

Sauce hachée – Take of chopped mushrooms and gherkins a spoonful each, half a spoonful of scalded minced parsley, with pepper, salt, and vinegar. Moisten with a little consommé, or with brown Italian sauce.

MARGARET DODS, *The Cook and Housewife's Manual*, 1826

A LA MODE BEEF

Dickens writes about visiting Johnson's famous à la mode beef house near London's Drury Lane, and this is where he has David Copperfield treat himself to a "small plate of that delicacy." An 1861 advert (now in the Museum of London) for Johnson's offers takeout (for working-class customers), a luncheon bar for "choicest viands," and "dinners sent out"—a service Dick Swiveller in *The Old Curiosity Shop* demands fruitlessly when he requires the nearest eating house to send "an immediate supply of boiled beef and greens."

SERVES 4

a little olive oil

2 onions, chopped

6 slices of streaky unsmoked bacon, chopped small

a pinch of freshly ground white pepper

½ teaspoon ground cloves

¼ teaspoon ground mace

¼ teaspoon ground nutmeg

top roast or silverside or other pot-roasting joint of beef, approx. 2 lb 3 oz/1kg

2¼ cups/500ml hot beef stock (or substitute about ¾ cup/200ml with white or red wine; or about 3½ tablespoons/50ml with brandy)

1 bay leaf

a few sprigs of thyme

Preheat the oven to 325°F/160°C/Gas 3.

Heat a little oil in a large skillet/frying pan and sauté the onions until transparent. Add the bacon and fry until the fat begins to color. Add the spices and stir for a couple of minutes. Transfer to a flameproof casserole, add the wine or brandy if using, and let it bubble and reduce.

Heat a little more oil in the skillet/frying pan, add the joint of beef, and brown all over.

Place the joint on top of the onion and spice mixture, pour the hot stock around it, add the herbs, and bring to a simmer.

Cover and cook in the preheated oven for about 2 hours, turning halfway, until the beef is very tender. Serve with greens and carrots.

BEEF A LA MODE IN PIECES

You must take a Buttock of Beef, cut it into two Pound Pieces, lard them with Bacon, fry them Brown, put them into a Pot that will just hold them, put in two Quarts of Broth or Gravy, a few Sweet Herbs, and Onion, some Mace, Cloves, Nutmeg, Pepper and Salt; when that is done, cover it close, and stew till it is tender, skim off all the Fat, lay the Meat in the Dish, and strain the sauce over it. You may serve it up hot or cold.

HANNAH GLASSE, *The Art of Cookery Made Plain and Easy*, 1747

MARROW PUDDING

In *Bleak House*, Smallweed unhesitatingly recommends Marrow Pudding to Guppy and Jobling for "pastry" in their dining house dinner. Queen Victoria had bone marrow every day for dinner, according to Francatelli, who suggests asking the butcher to break the bone for you as "this is rather an awkward affair for ladies." The chef of the renowned London Tavern, where Ralph Nickleby attends a public meeting, gives two recipes, here combined. The bone marrow gives it an unctuous, butterscotchy taste. Do try it.

SERVES 6

approx. 4–5 tablespoons/
60–75g butter or bone
marrow (ask your butcher
to split a large bone
lengthways)

8 slices of stale brioche
or white bread

butter, for greasing

²⁄₃ cup/150ml light/single
cream

¾ cup/200ml milk

3 eggs

3 tablespoons brandy

½ cup/50g candied/mixed
fruit (including cut mixed
peel)

1–2 tablespoons light
brown sugar

1 tablespoon demerara
sugar, mixed with
½ teaspoon grated nutmeg

Scrape out the bone marrow and chop it finely, or butter the bread.

Thickly butter a shallow 1¾-pint/1-litre baking dish and arrange half the bread (butter side up if you are not using bone marrow) in the bottom. Sprinkle half the bone marrow on top, if using.

Beat together the cream, milk, eggs, and brandy. Pour half of this onto the bread, sprinkle over most of the fruit and a tablespoon of light brown sugar (or more if you have a sweet tooth), and leave for 20 minutes or so for the mixture to soak in.

Preheat the oven to 350°F/180°C/Gas 4.

Put the remaining bread slices on top, butter side up if not using bone marrow, or butter side down and sprinkle the remainder of the marrow on top. Pour the remaining cream mixture evenly over the bread, and sprinkle the remaining fruit and the demerara sugar-nutmeg mixture on top.

Bake in the oven for 40–45 minutes. Eat while puffed up and hot.

MARROW PUDDING

Grate a penny loaf into crumbs, and pour on them a pint of boiling hot cream. Cut very thin a pound of beef marrow, beat four eggs well, and then add a glass of brandy, with sugar and nutmeg to your taste. Mix them all well together, and then boil or bake it. Three quarters of an hour will do it. Cut two ounces of citron very thin, and when you dish it up, stick them all over it.

JOHN FARLEY, *The London Art of Cookery*, 1783

EATING OUT

The introduction to *What Shall We Have for Dinner?* is generally agreed to be by Charles, rather than Catherine Dickens, writing as Lady Maria Clutterbuck. Looking back on her happy life with the late, well-fed Sir Jonas, she warns her female friends who have ruined domestic harmony with "a surplusage of cold mutton or a redundancy of chops" that their miscalculation makes "the Club more attractive than the Home." Mrs. Beeton agreed that "men are now so well served out of doors,—at their clubs, well-ordered taverns, and dining-houses" that if a woman wanted to see anything of her husband, she must not give him "the cold shoulder." Chefs, such as Alexis Soyer, gained their celebrity in the kitchens of private members' clubs (where, naturally, ladies were not admitted as members). His Reform Club kitchen was famous for its modern equipment and excellent food. Public restaurants and taverns were also generally for men, but there were private rooms for accompanied women and private parties. Genteel women ate with one another on home visits.

Dickens invited friends to join him for seafood in taverns at Greenwich and Blackwall, on the Thames estuary. He also hosted sizeable dinners upriver in leafy Richmond; here, at the Star and Garter, the guests at a publication dinner for *David Copperfield* included Alfred, Lord Tennyson and William Thackeray. Dickens also began to entertain at the office of *Household Words*, effectively cutting Catherine out of parties such as "a gipsy sort of cold dinner" of pickled salmon and cold pigeon pie, to which he invited the painter Frank Stone (letter, July 22, 1851) and the journalist Mark Lemon and his wife. In these instances he ordered in food from a hotel in York Street, Covent Garden. Inns operated a takeout service— Mr. Pumblechook, entertaining Pip to dinner in *Great Expectations* when he believes him to be wealthy, offers him a chicken and tongue and other dainties, all "had round from the Boar."

Dickens's novels are famously full of inns that, no matter what peculiarities and devilry the patrons get up to, are cheerful and hospitable. The Maypole Inn of *Barnaby Rudge* was "the snuggest, cosiest, and completest bar that ever the wit of man devised." Of the many Pickwickian pubs, The George and Vulture is "good, old-fashioned and comfortable," while The Marquis of Granby, owned by Mr. Weller senior, is large enough to be convenient and small enough to be snug, with

Guppy's Dining House Treat

The Crown & Sceptre was one
of many inns on the banks of the
Thames at Greenwich, to the
south-east of the city of London

geraniums and a well-dusted row of spirit phials. The popularity of inns put them into an interesting position vis à vis social class. Herbert Pocket, teaching Pip the ways of the genteel world in *Great Expectations*, tells him that a gentleman may not on any account keep a public house, "but a public-house may keep a gentleman."

Dickens' restlessness ensured that he sampled taverns across the country, and indeed on his travels in Europe and America. Dinners at staging inns—crucial punctuation points for long and unheated journeys by stagecoach—locate his characters in a past era as rail travel took over. The railroads were universally agreed to provide bad food and worse service; in *The Uncommercial Traveller* (1860s), Dickens books himself into a railway Refreshment Station to encounter a defiant and resentful waitress, a windtrap of a room, and "glutinous lumps of gristle and grease, called pork-pie." As he eats hurriedly in a Terminus hotel, the inhospitable and shambling waiter eventually produces a veal cutlet with a "sort of fur" on its surface, served with "a cutaneous kind of sauce of brown pimples" (*Refreshments for Travellers*, March 24, 1860). He must have thought longingly of the lobster salad picnics he provided for the Pickwick Club, or the one that Sam Weller details as he unpacks the basket—"Tongue; well that's a wery good thing when it an't a woman's. Bread—knuckle o'ham, reg'lar picter—cold beef in slices, wery good."

PICKLED SALMON

Mrs. Gamp, in *Martin Chuzzlewit*, settles in to nurse her patient by taking his pillows and ordering in "a little bit of pickled salmon, with a nice little sprig of fennel, and a sprinkling of white pepper...." Londoners loved "Newcastle pickled salmon," but Dickens is amused to discover (in his re-write of Grimaldi's memoirs, 1838) that it was "an article unknown in Newcastle, all Newcastle pickled salmon being sent to London for sale."

SERVES 4 AS A MAIN COURSE
OR 8 AS AN APPETIZER

1¼ cups/300ml good-quality white wine vinegar

1¼ cups/300ml water

3 red onions, peeled and sliced

1 turnip, peeled, quartered, and roughly chopped

a bunch of flat-leaf parsley and thyme (tied together)

1 bay leaf

½ teaspoon salt

2–3 teaspoons sugar

12 whole white peppercorns, slightly crushed

1 lb 2 oz/500g salmon fillets, skinned

a handful of dill

For the dressing

reserved marinade

olive oil

Dijon or wholegrain mustard

To serve

sprigs of fennel, fennel flowers, or dill

To make the marinade, put all the ingredients except the salmon and dill in a saucepan and bring to the boil. Simmer for 10–15 minutes, then put through a strainer/sieve, keeping the marinade.

If you wish, reserve 4–7 tablespoons/50–100ml of the marinade for a salad dressing.

If you wish to poach the salmon, put the strained marinade back in the pan, lower the fish into it, and let it simmer gently for 8–10 minutes, then set aside to cool.

For salmon that is a little raw and soft in the middle, place the salmon fillets in a glass or ceramic dish in a single layer and pour the hot marinade over them. Set aside to cool.

When the liquid is tepid, add the dill to the marinade. Chill in the fridge for 2 hours.

Remove the salmon from the marinade. Using a sharp knife, slice the fish thinly. Arrange on a plate, decorated with fennel sprigs, fennel flowers, or dill.

Serve with Betsey Prig's Twopenny Salad (see page 70). For a dressing, whisk the reserved marinade together with olive oil (in the ratio of 3 parts oil to 1 part marinade) and a little mustard.

TROUT A LA TWICKENHAM

The remains of trout, salmon, or mackerel, are excellent pickled: – put three onions in slices in a stewpan, with two ounces of butter, one turnip, a bouquet of parsley, thyme, and bay-leaf, pass them five minutes over the fire, add a pint of water and a pint of vinegar, two teaspoonfuls of salt and one of pepper, boil until the onions are tender, then strain it through a sieve over the fish; it will keep some time if required, and then do to pickle more fish by boiling over again.

ALEXIS SOYER, *The Modern Housewife or Ménagère,* 1849

BETSEY PRIG'S TWOPENNY SALAD

When Mrs. Gamp invites her friend Betsey Prig to tea, "two pounds of Newcastle salmon, intensely pickled" is on the menu; Mrs. Prig contributes as much salad as she can fit into her pocket, consisting of "either the oldest of lettuces or youngest of cabbages," shut up like an umbrella, mustard and cress, dandelion, radish, onion, beets/beetroot, and celery. Catherine also served beetroot and celery salads year round.

SERVES 4 AS A MAIN COURSE
OR 8 AS AN APPETIZER

crisp lettuce such as Little Gem or Romaine

endive, chicory, radicchio, arugula/rocket, or young dandelions or similar bitter leaves

6–8 radishes, thinly sliced

2–3 medium beets/beetroot, freshly boiled or baked, peeled and chopped into small cubes

4–6 salad onions or chives, finely chopped

4–5 stalks of heart celery, finely chopped

mustard and cress or soft herbs such as flat-leaf parsley or cilantro/coriander

salad dressing, made with 5 parts oil to 2 parts cucumber or tarragon vinegar, plus salt and pepper (and optional sugar to taste)

Make the vinegar for the dressing by steeping cucumber or tarragon in good white wine vinegar or cider vinegar for around 3 hours.

Wash all the salad leaves and refresh in cold water if necessary. Shred the leaves and toss with the radish onto a salad bowl or plate. Sprinkle the chopped beet/beetroot, salad onions, and celery over. Decorate with chopped herbs or mustard and cress, and dress just before serving.

ENGLISH SALADS

The herbs and vegetables for a salad cannot be too freshly gathered; they should be carefully cleared from insects and washed with scrupulous nicety; they are better when not prepared until near the time of sending them to table, and should not be sauced until the instant before they are served.

Tender lettuces, of which the stems should be cut off, and the outer leaves be stripped away, mustard and cress, young radishes, and occasionally chives or small green onions (when the taste of a party is in favour of these last) are the usual ingredients of summer salads. (In early spring, the young white leaves of the dandelion will supply a very wholesome and excellent salad, of which the slight bitterness is to many persons as agreeable as that of the endive.) Half-grown cucumbers sliced thin, and mixed with them are a favourite addition with many persons. In England it is customary to cut the lettuces extremely fine; the French, who object to the flavour of the knife, which they fancy this mode imparts, break them small instead. Young celery alone, sliced and dressed with a rich salad mixture, is excellent; it is still in some families served thus always with roast pheasants.

Beet root, baked or boiled, blanched endive, small salad-herbs which are easily raised at any time of the year, celery, and hardy lettuces, with any ready-dressed vegetable, will supply salads through the winter. Cucumber vinegar is an agreeable addition to these.

ELIZA ACTON, *Modern Cookery for Private Families*, 1845

CHAPTER 5

A Little Tea

Martin Chuzzlewit

◆

Let Us Be Merry
Fred Barnard

One moonlit evening, Martin Chuzzlewit is welcomed as apprentice and lodger at Mr. Pecksniff's, where his two daughters lay on sandwiches, acidic currant wine, dry captain's biscuits, and a "highly geological home-made cake." The household call this his "Installation Banquet," although the menu is what we would now call afternoon or high tea. Inviting guests to tea was the perfect way to be genteel, without the expense of a dinner. In *Bleak House*, the Snagsbys set out the best tea service for a "dainty" and "delicate" little six o'clock feast of fresh bread and butter, ham, anchovies, new-laid eggs, and hot buttered toast.

Throughout the nineteenth century, fashion—and the desire to be seen as sophisticated—pushed the dinner hour back later in the day. When the Pecksniffs stay at Todger's boarding house, the usual two o'clock dinner "was postponed until five, in order that everything might be as genteel as the occasion demanded." The "afternoon tea" that was "invented" by Lady Bedford in 1840 didn't make it into *Mrs. Beeton's Book of Household Management* until 1880, and tea and cakes were generally taken after dinner. Martin Chuzzlewit, discomposed by the speed of dinner in an American boarding house, is revived by an English-style after-dinner tea with "cunning tea-cakes and sweet preserves" and the company of two pretty young ladies. And Mr. Pecksniff, in spite of dining—and drinking—well at Mrs. Todger's, still takes coffee and a muffin after dinner.

Toasting muffins, crumpets, and bread against the fire made them the centerpiece of a cozy tea. Muffins could be bought in the streets or delivered to your door—a 14-year-old muffin-man told Henry Mayhew, "We're a great conwenience to the ladies, sir, as likes a slap-up tea...." (as cited in "Of Muffin and Crumpet-selling in the Streets," in *London Labour and the London Poor*). Tea-drinking soared in England after its taxation was slashed in 1784, and it draws Dickensian characters together in innumerable intimate scenes—even Mr. Bumble in *Oliver Twist* is allowed sweet tea and buttered toast and to kiss Mrs. Corney.

HIGHLY GEOLOGICAL HOMEMADE CAKE

The Misses Pecksniff may not have intended a stratified cake for Martin's Installation Banquet, but fancy layered cakes were popular. An American fan invented the Dolly Varden cake, with chocolate, white, pink, and yellow layers, after the flamboyant character in *Barnaby Rudge*. The name now describes little girls' birthday cakes in the shape of fairy princesses.

SERVES 8–10

1½ cups plus 2 teaspoons/350g butter, softened, plus extra for greasing

1¾ cups/350g granulated/caster sugar

6 eggs, well beaten

2⅔ cups/350g self-rising flour

For the four flavors

zest of 1 orange and 2 tablespoons carrot juice, plus 1 extra tablespoon flour

2 tablespoons raspberry, redcurrant, or blackcurrant juice

zest of 1 lemon and juice of half, plus 1 extra tablespoon flour (or leave this layer plain)

2 oz/50g plain chocolate, melted in a bowl over a pan of hot water

For the chocolate frosting

2 oz/50g milk or plain chocolate, broken into small pieces

1¾ tablespoons/25g butter

1⅔ cups/225g confectioners'/ icing sugar

1 egg white

crystallized rose petals (optional)

You may find it easier to make this in two batches of two cakes, particularly if you have only two cake pans/tins.

Preheat the oven to 375°F/190°C/Gas 5. Grease four round 7-inch/18-cm cake pans/tins.

Cream the butter and sugar together until pale and fluffy. Add the eggs a very little at a time, beating well after each addition. If your mixture separates, stabilize it by adding a little of the flour. Fold in the flour with a metal spoon.

Divide the mixture between four bowls and add the flavoring to each bowl. (If you would like the layers to have stronger colors, you can add a drop of orange or red food coloring to the relevant bowls.) Mix in gently, then transfer into the greased cake pans/tins and level the tops.

Bake in the preheated oven for 20 minutes. When the cakes are coming away from the side of the pan/tin, take them out of the oven and cool in the pan/tin on a wire rack.

When they are cool, remove from the pan/tin and use a sharp knife to cut off the outer edges so the colors are clearly visible.

To make the frosting, melt the chocolate in a bowl over a pan of simmering water. Add the butter and when it has melted, add the sugar and egg white. Keeping the bowl over the pan of simmering water, beat the frosting until it is smooth.

Place the bottom layer of cake on a serving plate and top with a layer of frosting. Repeat with the remaining cakes, carefully stacking them so the sides are level, and with frosting between the layers and on the top. If you wish, decorate the top with crystallized rose petals.

DOLLY VARDEN CAKE

One cup sugar, one-third cup butter, one-quarter cup milk, one full cup flour measured before sifting, whites of six eggs, one-quarter teaspoon soda, three-quarters cream tartar; bake half of this plain, the other half color with one-quarter teaspoon of confectioner's cochineal; flavor with rose water. Bake the same quantity of the receipt, using the yolks of the eggs, coloring one-half with one teacup of grated chocolate; bake in jelly tins; frost each layer with very thin frosting taking care not to get too much sugar; put together chocolate, whites, rose, and yellows. Very handsome and very good. Try it.

MRS. D.O. MORTON, *Melrose Household Treasure*, 1877

CUNNING TEA CAKES

Like Dickens, Martin Chuzzlewit is shocked by the uncouth speed of dinner at a New York boarding house. Tea "with sweet preserves, and cunning tea-cakes," and two pretty young ladies, restores him to a "highly genial state." Mrs. Rundell's tea cake is something between a biscuit and a scone, the "Fat Rascal" of a story Dickens published in his first edition of *All the Year Round*, and still loved in Yorkshire today.

MAKES ABOUT 6

1¾ cups/225g all-purpose/plain flour

2 level teaspoons baking powder

1 teaspoon apple pie spice/mixed spice or ¾ teaspoon ground cinnamon and ¼ teaspoon nutmeg

½ cup/110g butter, chilled and diced

⅓ cup/70g granulated/caster sugar, plus extra for sprinkling

1 cup/125g currants (or mixed with raisins and golden raisins/sultanas)

½ cup/55g chopped candied/mixed peel

1 egg plus 1 yolk, beaten

1 tablespoon brandy or full-fat/whole milk

zest of ½ lemon

To glaze

1 egg white, beaten

1 tablespoon granulated/caster sugar

Preheat the oven to 400°F/200°C/Gas 6. Grease or line two baking trays.

Sift the flour, baking powder, and spices together. Rub in the butter. Stir in the sugar, dried fruit, and peel.

Whisk the egg with the brandy or milk and lemon zest, add to the dry ingredients, and mix with a round-bladed knife to make a firm dough. Add more milk if the dough is too dry and crumbly.

Handling the dough as little as possible, tip it onto a floured board and pat into a circle about 1¼ inches/3cm thick; cut out rounds using a large cutter (3¼ or 4 inches/8 or 10cm). You should also get one or two extra tea cakes out of the trimmings. Glaze with egg white and sprinkle with sugar.

Slide on to the baking trays and bake for 15–20 minutes before transferring to a wire rack to cool a little. Eat warm with butter.

TEA CAKES

Rub fine four ounces of butter into eight ounces of flour; mix eight ounces of currants, and six of fine Lisbon sugar, two yolks and one white of eggs, and a spoonful of brandy. Roll the paste the thickness of an Oliver biscuit, and cut with a wine glass. You may beat the other white, and wash over them; and either dust sugar, or not, as you like.

MRS. RUNDELL, *A New System of Domestic Cookery*, 1806

THE DICKENSES ABROAD

Dickens was torn between yearning for a settled, comfortable domestic life and excitement and change—a desire he fulfilled, in the earlier part of his life, through traveling and living abroad.

Not yet age 30, but already famous on both sides of the Atlantic, he persuaded Catherine to leave their children behind in England for several months and join him on a trip to America. Setting off by steamship from Liverpool on January 3, 1842, he attempted to remedy her seasickness with brandy and hot water during the voyage to Boston. There he was honored with The Boz Ball, which featured a banquet for 2,500 people which included 50,000 oysters, 10,000 sandwiches, and 25 pyramid cakes; one costing $30 was decorated with a scene from *The Old Curiosity Shop*.

Dickens' account of the trip, *American Notes*, features a cheerful picnic he was given on Looking Glass Prairie, outside of St Louis, camping near a solitary log-house for the sake of its water. He was given familiar treats such as champagne, roast fowls, lemon and sugar for punch, and the novelty of buffalo's tongue, which he described as an exquisite dainty. He enjoyed being initiated into the mystery of "Gin Sling, Cocktail, Sangaree, Mint Julep, Sherry-cobbler, Timber Doodle and other rare drinks," and describes drinking mint julep all evening with Washington Irving and Philip Hone. Catherine includes a recipe for the American "Hominy" made with Indian corn in her book, and borrowed three others, including leg of mutton stuffed with oysters, from the American cookbook writer Sarah Josepha Hale. The country failed to live up to the Republic of Dickens' imagination, however, and *American Notes* and Martin Chuzzlewit's dismay with, for example, the way working Americans bolted their food marked a rift between him and his American fans that was only really repaired by his second reading tour, in 1867.

Dickens' other sortie into travel literature, *Pictures from Italy*, describes him relocating his entire family to Genoa, to take advantage of its lower cost of living. They traveled there in an enormous carriage, which Dickens christened his "Pantechnicon," and the trip is recycled in the second half of *Little Dorrit*. He was full of admiration for the Brave Courier who shepherded them on their journey, elbowed his way into the kitchens of their inns, and, in a whirlwind, produced hot and wholesome meals from unpromising ingredients. The Courier is honored in a

The Cunard ship "Britannia", on which Charles and Catherine Dickens sailed to America in 1842.

fictional counterpart, Miss Pross, in *A Tale of Two Cities*. In Soho with the Manettes, she learns French techniques from impoverished emigrés, so successfully that the English domestics regard her as a sorceress or Cinderella's godmother for changing "a fowl, a rabbit, a vegetable or two from the garden" into "anything she pleased."

Dickens particularly enjoyed French café culture and admired their habits of care and courtesy toward travelers. He ventriloquizes his experience of eating in the Refreshment Rooms on French railroads through Mrs. Lirriper, who exclaims that everything is "so civil and so hot and attentive and every way comfortable..." in great contrast to the "injured young women a glaring at you and grudging you" in the British equivalent (*Mrs. Lirriper's Legacy*).

Catherine missed Britain and its food more. From Genoa, Dickens wrote to his merchant friend, Mr. Thomas Curry, on August 9, 1844—"Catherine says she will take it as a great favour, if you will buy her, at your leisure and in the course of your own marketings, three pounds of black tea, and a Ham."

Catherine's menus are, on the whole, British. A single tomato appears in the whole book, accompanying a veal cutlet. By the time she had published the first edition and added more recipes to the 1854 edition, she had lived in Genoa (Italy), Lausanne (Switzerland), and Paris and Boulogne (France). French cuisine dominated fashionable dining in Britain, Italian dishes weren't unknown, and Anglo-Indian curries were commonly found on middle-class dinner tables. It is hard to unpick the influence of Catherine's travels on recipes such as Fondue or Timballe of Macaroni that she gives alongside her British stalwarts.

SANDWICHES

The sandwich became popular at all levels of Victorian society. In *The Pickwick Papers*, Sam Weller tells his father that clerks are all "eating Sandvidges" "Cos it's their dooty... it's a part o' the system." At Martin Chuzzlewit's "Installation Banquet," the sandwiches are "very long and very slim." Well-to-do Victorians liked unusual fillings in dainty finger sandwiches (tiny ones were called "thumb-bits") garnished and served on fancy napkins, to distinguish them from food eaten by workers.

Dandelion Sandwich

2–3 oz/60–80g cooked meat or fish, very finely chopped

a knob of softened butter

salt and freshly ground black pepper

2 slices of fresh white or brown bread

4–6 young dandelion leaves, washed

Mix the meat or fish with the butter, seasoning with salt and pepper. Spread on one side of the bread and lay the fresh dandelion leaves on top. Top with the remaining slice of bread.

Walnut Sandwich

1½–2 oz/40–60g Gruyère cheese, thinly sliced, or use creamy blue cheese (it keeps the walnuts in place and tastes better with the walnuts)

2 slices of fresh brown bread, buttered

25g/1 tablespoon crushed walnuts

Layer the cheese on one slice of bread, top with the walnuts, and press the buttered top slice down, to keep the walnuts in place. Serve with sherry and a green salad.

Indian Sandwich

2–3 oz/60–80g cooked pheasant or other game, finely chopped

1 teaspoon lime pickle

1 olive, finely chopped

½ whole anchovy, or 1 anchovy fillet, boned and finely chopped

2 teaspoons mayonnaise

2 slices of fresh brown or white bread

Mix all the filling ingredients together, spread on one slice of bread, and top with the remaining slice.

Shrimp Sandwich

2 oz/50g miniature shrimp

a knob of softened butter

salt and cayenne pepper

a splash of tarragon vinegar
or lemon juice

2 slices of fresh brown or
white bread

Mash the shrimp to a paste with the back of a fork, blending in the butter and a little salt and cayenne as you do so; add a small splash of tarragon vinegar or lemon juice. Spread on one slice of bread, and top with the remaining slice.

DANDELION SANDWICH

Pound the remains of any cold cooked meat, poultry, or fish, in a mortar, mix in a small quantity of butter while pounding, and season to taste. Pick and wash some Dandelion-leaves, dry them on a cloth, spread the mixture on some thin slices of bread-and-butter, put a few of the Dandelion-leaves on top, and cover over with more slices.

Cut the sandwiches into halves, quarters, triangles, or fingers, arrange them on a folded napkin or a fancy dish-paper, garnish with sprigs of parsley, and serve. For picnics, &c., these sandwiches are invaluable, as being cut a long time before using, they are liable to become dry, which the Dandelion-leaves prevent and make them more palatable.

THEODORE GARRETT, *The Encyclopaedia of Practical Cookery, Volume 3,* 1892-94

WALNUT SANDWICHES

Cut off very thin slices of home-made bread (trimming off the crust), lightly butter them, and upon each slice lay the thinnest possible slice of Gruyere cheese. Have ready peeled as many fresh Walnuts as will cover half of the slices, lay them upon the cheese, sprinkle a very little salt over them, cover with another thin shaving of cheese and more very thin buttered bread, press the slices of bread close together to hold the nuts in place, and serve the sandwiches with sherry wine; or they may be served with green salad, with plain salad dressing. These are an excellent after dinner relish.

THEODORE GARRETT, *The Encyclopaedia of Practical Cookery, Volume 8,* 1892-94

INDIAN SANDWICHES

Finely mince the white flesh of some cold pheasant, a small quantity of hot pickle, four olives and anchovies, the two latter ingredients should be well washed and the anchovies boned. Mix all these ingredients together with about 1 teacupful of mayonnaise sauce. Cut some thin slices of bread-and-butter, spread half of them over with the above mixture, and cover with the remaining half. Cut each slice into strips about 1in. wide, arrange them on a dish over which has been spread a folded napkin or a fancy dish-paper, garnish them with parsley, and serve.

THEODORE GARRETT, *The Encyclopaedia of Practical Cookery, Volume 6,* 1892-94

SHRIMP SANDWICHES

Pick a pint of Shrimps, put them in a mortar with 2oz. of butter, season with a little salt and cayenne pepper, and pound them to a paste; moisten it with a few drops of tarragon vinegar. Cut some rather thin slices of bread-and-butter, spread half of them with the paste, fold the remaining half over these, and press them lightly together. Cut the sandwiches into fingers or quarters, arrange them on a folded napkin or an ornamental dish-paper, garnish with parsley, and serve.

THEODORE GARRETT, *The Encyclopaedia of Practical Cookery, Volume 6,* 1892-94

CAPTAIN'S BISCUITS

Ships' biscuits or "hardtack" were flour and water baked hard to survive long voyages. Captain's biscuits at least had a little butter added, although Dickens jokes that they are "always a moist and jovial sort of viand." Very thin and crisp, they are ideal with cheese or potted fish. Add any kind of flavoring— black pepper, sea salt flakes, finely chopped herbs such as rosemary or chives, or seeds such as poppy or sesame.

MAKES ABOUT 36 BISCUITS

1½ cups/200g all-purpose/ plain flour

a pinch of salt

3½ tablespoons/50g cold butter

4–5 tablespoons cold milk or water

Preheat the oven to 350°F/180°C/Gas 4. Line two baking trays with baking parchment paper.

Sift the flour and a pinch of salt into a bowl. Dice the butter with a knife into the flour, then rub it in using your fingertips.

Add 4 tablespoons cold milk or water and mix to bind it together. Add a tiny bit more liquid if necessary—you need a dough that is pliable in the hands but dry enough to roll out easily.

Roll out as thinly as possible (about ⅛ inch/2mm thick), cut into rounds using cookie cutters or into squares with a knife. Prick the biscuits all over on one side with a fork. Transfer to the lined baking trays, pricked side down, and then prick the other side all over with a fork.

Bake in the preheated oven for 10–15 minutes until they are dry and golden. Transfer to a wire rack and leave to cool completely.

CAPTAIN'S BISCUITS

Rub ½ lb of butter into 7lb of fine sifted flour, and make into a dough with 1qt of water or milk, or a little more if required, taking every precaution to keep the dough as dry as consistent with adhesiveness. Break thoroughly, and roll out pieces of 4oz each to 4½ in in diameter; dock these, and lay them with their faces together. When the oven is ready, lay them on a baking-sheet, and bake quickly to a light brown.

THEODORE GARRETT, *The Encyclopaedia of Practical Cookery, Volume 1,* 1892-94

CHAPTER 6

Cakes for Giving

David Copperfield *and* The Mystery of Edwin Drood

—◆◆—

Steerforth and Mr. Mell
H.K. Browne (Phiz)

To dessert-lovers, Dickens' hurried mentions of the "tart" or "pudding" that round off a good meal can be a little frustrating. Savory roast meats and pies or alcoholic punches draw his attention and descriptions, whereas sweet things are often associated with childishness. Perhaps because *David Copperfield* is one of the most autobiographical of Dickens' novels, though, he remembers a boyish hunger for sugar and permits his characters to treat one another with some specific biscuits and cakes.

The "soft, seedy biscuits" that the romantic young David Copperfield secretly gives to his first crush were probably caraway biscuits. There is an almost identical gift in *The Pickwick Papers* when Ben Allen recalls his sister rejecting his friend Bob Sawyer's gift of "two small caraway-seed biscuits and one sweet apple," on the grounds that they were unpleasantly warm from being in the pocket of his corduroys—a location that suggests Dickens was playing on the association between seeds and fertility.

Newly at school, David is dazzled by the glamorous older boy Steerforth, and readily entrusts his only money to him so that Steerforth may buy their dormitory a midnight feast of currant wine and almond cakes, biscuits, and fruit. Steerforth is an interesting mixture of psychological acuteness—he gets the measure immediately of David's susceptibility and generosity—and still juvenile tastes. He exploits David's innocence to satisfy his own appetites—as he does later in the novel, when he seduces and then abandons Little Em'ly.

David's aunt Betsey Trotwood treats her childlike, innocent, and loyal friend Mr. Dick to the gingerbread that he is "very partial" to. The Reverend Septimus Crisparkle in *The Mystery of Edwin Drood* is also a "boy-like" man who can be cheered up by something delicious from his mother's "most wonderful closet," full of jams and pickles, Constantia wine and cordials, homemade biscuits, plum cakes, and ladies' finger biscuits.

ALMOND CAKE FOR STEERFORTH

The feast of currant wine, biscuits, fruit, and almond cakes that Steerforth persuades David Copperfield to provide feeds David's infatuation with the charismatic older boy. A subsequent gift from Peggotty, of cake, oranges, and cowslip wine, he lays at the feet of Steerforth for him to dispense. William Kitchiner's light almond cake pairs well with oranges, berries, or other fruit.

SERVES 8–10

butter, for greasing

5 free-range eggs

1 cup minus 1 tablespoon/180g golden superfine/caster sugar (or granulated sugar, if you cannot find golden superfine/caster sugar)

finely grated zest of 1 lemon or orange

1 teaspoon almond extract (optional)

a pinch of salt

a pinch of cream of tartar

2 cups/200g ground almonds

¼ cup/35g all-purpose/plain flour

For the frosting

1 tablespoon orange or lemon juice

¾ cup/100g confectioners'/icing sugar, sifted

To serve

fresh fruit, such as raspberries or cherries, or fruit compôte, such as orange, apricot, or plum (see page 91)

Preheat the oven to 350°F/180°C/Gas 4. Grease a 9-inch/23-cm bundt pan/tin or ring mold, or a plain springform pan/tin.

Separate the eggs and leave the whites to come to room temperature. Make sure there is no yolk or fat in the whites, which would prevent them from beating properly.

Beat the yolks with ½ cup/100g of the sugar until pale and fluffy, then beat in the lemon or orange zest and the almond extract, if using.

In a completely clean bowl, beat the egg whites until stiff (you should be able to turn the bowl upside down and they won't fall out!). Add a quarter of the remaining sugar, the pinch of salt, and the cream of tartar, beat again, then fold in the rest of the sugar.

Fold the whites into the batter, a quarter at a time, followed by the almonds and flour. Scrape the mixture into the mold or pan. Bake in the preheated oven for 35–40 minutes until the cake is shrinking from the sides of the pan.

Remove from the oven and leave the cake to cool in the pan for 10 minutes, then turn it out.

To make the frosting, stir the orange or lemon juice into the sifted confectioner's/icing sugar, then drizzle over the cake. Fill the center of the cake with fresh fruit such as raspberries or cherries. Alternatively, keep it plain and serve it with a compôte of fruit such as oranges, apricots, or plums.

ALMOND SPONGE CAKE

Pound in a mortar one pound of blanched Almonds quite fine, with the Whites of three Eggs, then put in one pound of sifted Loaf-Sugar, some grated Lemon-peel, and the Yolks of fifteen Eggs, work them well together: beat up to a solid froth the Whites of twelve Eggs, and stir them into the other Ingredients with a quarter of a pound of sifted dry Flour: prepare a mould; put in the mixture, and bake it an hour in a slow oven; take it carefully from the mould, and set it on a sieve.

WILLIAM KITCHINER, *Apicius Redivivus, or The Cook's Oracle*, 1817

COMPÔTES OF FRUIT

Eliza Acton recommends a compôte of fruit as a more elegant dessert than the "common 'stewed fruit' of English cookery." The fruit, being added to a syrup, better retains its structure and taste, and the syrup is beautifully translucent. She recommends serving the redcurrant compôtes with the substantial batter, custard, bread, or ground rice puddings Victorians loved. It would also go beautifully with the almond cake (see page 88) or gruel (see page 128).

Eliza Acton recommends the following proportions and timings:

Rhubarb, gooseberries, cherries, damsons—syrup made from ¾ cup/140g sugar with 1¼ cups/280ml water; add 1 lb/450g fruit and simmer for about 10 minutes.

Redcurrants and raspberries—syrup made from ¾ cup/140g sugar with ⅔ cup/140ml water; add 1 lb/450g fruit and simmer for 5–7 minutes.

Mrs. Beeton recommends the following proportions and timings:

Oranges—syrup made from 1½ cups/300g sugar with 2⅓ cups/570ml water; add 6 oranges, skin and pith removed, cut into segments. Simmer for 5 minutes.

Apples—syrup made from 1 cup plus 2 tablespoons/225g sugar to scant 1¼ cups/280ml water; peel, halve, and core the apples and simmer in the syrup with the juice and rind of a lemon for 15–25 minutes.

The preparation is simple. Gently boil white granulated sugar and water together for 10 minutes to make a syrup, skimming any scum from the surface. Add the fruit and simmer until the fruit is lightly cooked. If the syrup is too runny, remove the fruit with a slotted spoon and arrange it in a serving dish. Reduce the syrup over a medium heat, let it cool slightly, and then pour it over. It may also be served cold, and it keeps for a day or two in the fridge.

Cinnamon, cloves, vanilla beans/pods, or a little orange or lemon peel can be used as flavorings when you make the syrup.

MR DICK'S GINGERBREAD

Betsey Trotwood directs David Copperfield to open an account at a cake shop so that the childlike Mr. Dick might be treated to his favorite gingerbread on credit—but only up to one shilling per day. Both cake and biscuit gingerbreads were traditionally decorated as Christmas treats and the cloves in Eliza Acton's recipe hark back to the gilded cloves that ornamented medieval gingerbread.

SERVES 10-12

4 eggs

4 tablespoons milk

scant 3½ cups/450g self-rising flour

1 heaped tablespoon ground ginger (ground ginger loses its flavor rapidly, so buy in small quantities and use up quickly)

1 teaspoon ground cloves

⅞ cup/280g molasses/black treacle

⅞ cup/280g corn syrup/golden syrup

¾ cup plus 2 tablespoons/175g soft brown or muscovado sugar

¾ cup/170g butter, plus extra for greasing

zest of 2 lemons or oranges

2–3 tablespoons chopped stem ginger (optional)

Preheat the oven to 325°F/170°C/Gas 3. Grease and line a 9-inch/23-cm square cake pan/tin.

Whisk the eggs thoroughly with the milk, until they start to froth. Sift the flour and spices into a large bowl. Measure the molasses/black treacle and syrup into a saucepan (this is easiest to do using a metal spoon heated in hot water). Add the sugar, butter, and zest. Heat very gently until the butter is just melted. Pour this into a well in the flour, beating vigorously. When it is well blended, add the egg and milk mixture and the stem ginger, if using, beating well until you can see bubbles forming on the surface.

Pour into the prepared cake pan/tin and bake in the preheated oven for about 1½ hours until firm to the touch and a skewer inserted into the center comes out clean. Turn out and cool on a wire rack. Store in an airtight container or wrapped in foil for a day or two before eating to let the flavors develop.

ACTON GINGERBREAD

Whisk four strained or well-cleared eggs to the lightest possible froth and pour to them, by degrees, a pound and a quarter of treacle, still beating them lightly. Add, in the same manner, six ounces of pale brown sugar free from lumps, one pound of sifted flour, and six ounces of good butter, just sufficiently warmed to be liquid, and no more, for if hot, it would render the cake heavy; it should be poured in small portions to the mixture, which should be well beaten up with the back of a wooden spoon as each portion is thrown in: the success of the cake depends almost entirely on this part of the process. When properly mingled with the mass, the butter will not be perceptible on the surface; and if the cake be kept light by constant whisking, large bubbles will appear in it to the last. When it is so far ready, add to it one ounce of Jamaica ginger and a large teaspoonful of cloves in fine powder, with the lightly grated rinds of two fresh full-sized lemons.

Butter thickly, in every part, a shallow square tin pan, and bake the gingerbread slowly for nearly or quite an hour in a gentle oven. Let it cool a little before it is turned out, and set it on its edge until cold, supporting it, if needful, against a large jar or bowl. We have usually had it baked in an American oven, in a tin less than two inches deep; and it has been excellent. We retain the name given to it originally in our own circle.

ELIZA ACTON, *Modern Cookery for Private Families*, 1845

DAVID COPPERFIELD'S SOFT, SEEDY BISCUITS

The young David Copperfield offers "soft, seedy biscuits" to Miss Shepherd, a little girl with "a round face and curly flaxen hair," as a love token; while in *The Pickwick Papers* Bob Sawyer, with "all the eagerness of a child's love," presses upon Arabella Allen "two small caraway-seed biscuits." The seed, much loved by the Victorians as a flavoring, had an ancient reputation as an aphrodisiac.

MAKES 15–18

½ cup plus 1 tablespoon/125g unsalted butter, softened, plus extra for greasing

6 tablespoons/75g soft light brown sugar, plus extra for dusting

grated rind from ½ a lemon (optional—although not in the original recipe, this works well with poppy seeds)

1 free-range egg, separated

2 tablespoons seeds—caraway, poppy, or a mixture

1½ cups/200g all-purpose/plain flour

a pinch of salt

¼ teaspoon baking powder

1 tablespoon milk

Preheat the oven to 400°F/200°C/Gas 6. Grease or line two baking trays.

Beat the butter until creamy; beat in the sugar and lemon zest (if using) until pale and fluffy. Add the egg yolk and beat until well combined, then stir in the seeds. Sift in the flour, salt, and baking powder and combine to make a stiff dough. Add a very little milk if it is too crumbly. Roll out on a floured work surface to a thickness of ¼ inch/5mm. Cut out using a round 2 or 2½-inch/5 or 6-cm cutter, or a heart-shaped one if you wish, re-rolling the trimmings until all the dough is used. Place on the baking trays and bake in the preheated oven for 8–10 minutes until lightly baked and pale gold.

Remove from the oven, brush with a little beaten egg white, and sprinkle with the extra sugar. Return to the oven and cook for a further 3–5 minutes.

Cool on the baking trays until you can handle them, then remove to a wire rack to cool.

SEED BISCUITS

Ingredient – 1lb of flour, ¼ lb of sifted sugar, ¼ lb of butter, ½ oz caraway seeds, 3 eggs.

Mode – Beat the butter to a cream; stir in the flour, sugar, and caraway seeds; and when these ingredients are well mixed, add the eggs, which should be well whisked. Roll out the paste, with a round cutter shape out the biscuits, and bake them in a moderate oven from 10 to 15 minutes. The tops of the biscuits may be brushed over with a little milk or the white of an egg, and then a little sugar strewn over.

Time 10 to 15 minutes. *Average cost* 1s.

Sufficient to make 3 dozen biscuits. *Seasonable* at any time.

MRS. BEETON'S *Book of Household Management*, 1861

HOMEMADE BISCUITS

Wine and biscuits were often served together to revive the weary or troubled. In *The Mystery of Edwin Drood*, Mrs. Crisparkle, the Reverend Septimus' mother, rallies him with a glass of the sweet South African Constantia and a homemade biscuit, while in *Nicholas Nickleby* Miss La Creevy won't send Smike on his way without "a sip of something comfortable and a mixed biscuit." The orange, almonds, and seeds in Margaret Dods' shortbread recipe make it a perfect partner for dessert wine.

MAKES ABOUT 8

½ cup minus
1 tablespoon/100g
unsalted butter, softened

¼ cup/50g soft brown
sugar

1⅓ cups/180g all-
purpose/plain flour

¼ cup/25g finely chopped
almonds

⅙ cup/25g candied/
mixed peel

1 tablespoon caraway
seeds

Preheat the oven to 325°F/170°C/Gas 3. Line a baking tray with baking parchment paper.

Cream the butter and sugar together until thoroughly combined. Sift the flour in, working it in with a wooden spoon (you may find using your hands easier).

When it is mixed but not yet a dough, add the chopped almonds and peel, pressing and kneading until it comes together.

Form the dough into a round (or any shape you like). Place on the lined baking tray, then decorate the edge with a fork and score it into fingers or segments. Sprinkle caraway seeds on the top. Bake in the preheated oven for about 25–30 minutes until firm but still very pale.

When the shortbread has cooled, cut along the scored lines and store in an airtight container.

SCOTCH SHORT-BREAD

To the fourth of a peck of flour, take six ounces of sifted sugar and of candied citron and orange peel, and blanched almonds, two ounces each. Cut these in rather large slices, and mix them with the flour. Rub down among the flour a pound of butter in very minute bits, and melt a half-pound more, and with this work up the flour, &c. The less kneading it gets the more short and crisp the cakes will be. Roll out the paste into a large well-shaped oval cake, about an inch and a half thick, and divide this the narrow way, so as to have two cakes somewhat the shape of a Gothic arch. Pinch the cakes neatly at the edges, and mark them on the top with the instrument used for the purpose, or with a fork. Strew caraway-comfits over the top, and a few strips of citron peel. Bake on paper rubbed with flour. The cakes may be squares, or oblong figures.

MARGARET DODS, *The Cook and Housewife's Manual*, 1826

~ LADIES' FINGERS ~

Also known as savoy biscuits, Savoiardi, and sponge fingers, these are the unecclesiastical-sounding "various slender ladies' fingers, to be dipped into sweet wine and kissed" that the Reverend Septimus' mother finds in her most wonderful closet in *The Mystery of Edwin Drood* whenever that gentleman needs cheering up. Traditionally piped into fingers and used for Charlotte Russe (see page 150), they can also be piped into loose shapes.

MAKES ABOUT 20

¾ cup/150g granulated/caster sugar

zest of 1 lemon

4 eggs, separated

1 cup plus 2 tablespoons/150g all-purpose/plain flour

a pinch of cream of tartar (or a few drops of lemon juice)

½ teaspoon baking powder

2–3 tablespoons golden superfine/caster sugar, for sprinkling

Preheat the oven to 380°F/190°C/Gas 5. Line three baking trays with baking parchment paper.

Add the sugar and lemon zest to the egg yolks. Beat well until pale gold. Sift the flour into the egg yolks and fold in well.

Add the cream of tartar to the egg whites and whisk until stiff (the acid in the cream of tartar helps them keep their stiffness—if you don't have it, you could use a few drops of lemon juice); fold them into the yolk mixture.

Put the mixture into a piping bag fitted with a ¼-inch/5-mm nozzle and pipe 3–4-inch/8–10-cm lengths on the paper. Sprinkle golden caster sugar over the fingers.

Bake in the preheated oven for 15 minutes until they are pale golden (but check after 10 minutes as they burn quickly).

Slide a knife under the fingers while they are still hot to make sure they don't stick to the paper; after they have cooled for 2–3 minutes, transfer to a wire rack.

Serve with tea or use them for Charlotte Russe (see page 150). Your Ladies' Fingers will probably be flatter and softer than the store-bought variety (which are made in molds). If you are using them for a Charlotte Russe, you may wish to line them up on a board and trim them so they are all the same width and length; although it doesn't look quite as pretty, this makes the Charlotte Russe easier to assemble.

SAVOY BISCUITS OR CAKES

INGREDIENTS – *4 eggs, 6 oz of pounded sugar, the rind of 1 lemon, 6 oz of flour.*

MODE – *Break the eggs into a basin, separating the whites from the yolks; beat the yolks well, mix with them the pounded sugar and grated lemon-rind, and beat these ingredients together for ¼ hour. Then dredge in the flour gradually, and when the whites of the eggs have been whisked to a solid froth, stir them to the flour, &c; beat the mixture well for another 5 minutes, then draw it along in strips upon thick cartridge paper to the proper size of the biscuit, and bake them in rather a hot oven; but let them be carefully watched, as they are soon done, and a few seconds over the proper time will scorch and spoil them. These biscuits, or ladies'-fingers, as they are called, are used for making Charlotte Russes, and for a variety of fancy sweet dishes.*

TIME – *5 to 8 minutes, in a quick oven.*

AVERAGE COST – *1s, 8d, per lb, or ½d each.*

MRS. BEETON'S *Book of Household Management,* 1861

CHAPTER 7

A Tale of Two Christmases

Great Expectations *and* A Christmas Carol

The Ghost of Christmas Present Appears before Ebenezer Scrooge
John Leech

Dickens loved Christmas more than any other time of the year, as his eldest daughter, Mamie, recollected. He is often credited with "inventing" our Christmas dinner, and there is some truth in this. A *Christmas Carol*, published in 1843, was so influential that it anchored popular elements of Christmas food to the day itself.

Many Victorian families, like the Cratchits, ate plum pudding at Christmas, but it wasn't until two years after *A Christmas Carol* was published that the Dickens-loving Eliza Acton became the first to give her recipe the name of "Christmas Pudding." The Cratchits' goose would have been raised in a suburban "goose-club" or driven to London markets from East Anglia. The meatier turkey, not adapted to either practice, was reserved for the wealthy, until rail transport and refrigeration made it more readily available.

Pip's agonizing Christmas dinner in *Great Expectations* is an old-fashioned, rural Christmas feast of roast, stuffed fowls and a leg of pickled pork. Pigs and other livestock were usually slaughtered in the fall (winter fodder was scarce, so only some were kept for breeding). Pork was cured—salted or smoked, or both—in order to last the winter ("pickled" is another name for salted pork). The "beautiful, round, compact pork pie" that Pip has stolen for the convict Magwitch, and that is excitedly anticipated by Mrs. Joe, would have contained the last fresh pork of the year. The Gargerys' old-fashioned mince pie was likely to include chopped meat such as tongue or mutton, as Christmas "pyes" had done since Tudor times. This was going out of fashion, although suet was—and still is—an indispensable ingredient in mince pies.

Another old-fashioned part of Christmas celebrations was Twelfth Night— a more riotous and secular celebration than Christmas, with a tradition of play-acting that appealed to Dickens. Twelfth Cakes themselves were theatrical creations, decorated with showy figures and scenes in colored sugarpaste and snow-white confectionery.

ROAST GOOSE

Poor families would ensure that they got their Christmas goose by paying into a goose club and, without an oven, having it roasted by the baker. In *A Christmas Carol*, the Cratchit children go wild outside the bakery at the smell of sage-and-onion stuffing, and the whole family admire their goose's flavor (and cheapness); Mrs. Cratchit ekes it out with apple sauce and mashed potatoes. A turkey, costlier and harder to buy in cities, is what the reformed Scrooge treats the Cratchit family to.

SERVES 8–10

1 goose, about 11–13½ lb/5–6kg (with giblets and neck)

1 onion, peeled

a few sprigs of sage or thyme

To serve

potatoes and/or root vegetables, for roasting alongside the goose

unsweetened apple sauce/stewed apple

For the stuffing

2 large onions, finely chopped

3 tablespoons freshly chopped sage

4 cups/200g stale breadcrumbs

a little salt and freshly ground black pepper

2 free-range eggs

a little hot stock

For the gravy

goose neck, chopped

goose wings

1 carrot, roughly chopped

1 onion, roughly chopped

giblets

2 bay leaves

6 peppercorns

1 tablespoon all-purpose/plain flour

Preheat the oven to 400°F/200°C/Gas 6.

Chop off the wings and keep these for the stock. Pull out all the fat from inside the bird and cut off any extra visible fat. (Melt this fat gently in a saucepan, then strain it through a fine strainer/sieve or muslin. Keep in a jar in the fridge to roast vegetables or lean meat, such as rabbit.)

To make the stuffing, sweat the onions in a little of the goose fat until they are translucent. Add the sage, breadcrumbs, and seasoning, and bind with the eggs and a few spoonfuls of hot stock—the mixture should be moist enough to bind together but not at all sloppy. You can cook the stuffing separately if you prefer (see page 104 for instructions). If you are using it to stuff the goose, you will need to weigh the stuffing first.

Using a sharp skewer or knife, prick the skin of the bird all over, without going into the meat below (this will help the fat to run off). Rub salt into the skin and the cavity of the goose, and put either the peeled onion and sprigs of sage or thyme, or the stuffing, into the cavity.

To calculate the cooking time, add the weight of the stuffing to the weight of the bird if you are cooking the two together; cook for 15 minutes per 1 lb/450g plus 15 minutes; add 30 minutes' resting time.

Place the goose on a wire rack above a tray and roast in the preheated oven for the required time. Baste from time to time with the fat that collects in the tray. If the goose browns too quickly, cover the breast with foil.

Meanwhile, make the stock for the gravy by frying the chopped neck and wings and vegetables in a little goose fat in a large pan. Pour off any excess fat, add the giblets, bay leaves, and peppercorns and 1¾ pints/1 litre water. Let this simmer for 1½ hours, then strain and set aside.

When you are ready to roast your potatoes and vegetables (about 30 minutes before the goose comes out of the oven), pour out the fat from the tray, leaving enough for roasting (either take the goose out and put it on a board, holding it with two clean dish towels, or put another tray temporarily underneath, so the fat doesn't drip onto the floor of your oven). Continue to roast the goose on the rack with the vegetables in the tray below.

If you are cooking the stuffing separately, place it in a gratin dish and cook in the oven for 30 minutes.

When the goose is cooked through and the juices run clear, transfer it to a large plate, cover with foil, and let it rest for 20–30 minutes before carving.

To make the gravy, thicken the juices in the roasting tray with a little flour over a low heat, and slowly add the strained stock. Pour into a gravy boat.

Serve with unsweetened apple sauce/stewed apple.

ROAST GOOSE WITH SAGE AND ONION STUFFING

When a goose is well picked, singed, and cleaned, make the stuffing with about two ounces of onion and half as much green sage, chop them very fine, adding four ounces, i.e. about a large breakfast-cupful of stale bread-crumbs, a bit of butter about as big as a walnut, and a very little pepper and salt (to this some cooks add half the liver, parboiling it first); the yolk of an egg or two, and incorporating the whole well together, stuff the goose; do not quite fill it, but leave a little room for the stuffing to swell; spit it, tie it on the spit at both ends, to prevent its swinging round, and to keep the stuffing from coming out. From an hour and a half to an hour and three-quarters, will roast a fine full-grown goose. Send up gravy and apple sauce with it.

WILLIAM KITCHINER, *Apicius Redivivus, or The Cook's Oracle*, 1817

CHRISTMAS PUDDING

Plum puddings were ideal for special occasions; even the poor who had no oven could boil one up in the washing copper, like Mrs. Cratchit. Eliza Acton had almost certainly read *A Christmas Carol*; two years after it was published she was the first to rename plum pudding "Christmas Pudding." Her recipe is still recommended by modern cookery writers for being both light and rich.

SERVES 6–8

1²/₃ cups/170g grated suet (ask your butcher for approx. 7 oz/200g fresh beef-kidney suet)

²/₃ cup/85g all-purpose/ plain flour

a small pinch of salt

1½ cups/85g fresh white breadcrumbs

¾ cup/140g soft brown sugar

½ teaspoon apple pie spice/ mixed spice

1½ cups/170g raisins

1½ cups/170g currants

¾ cup/55g chopped candied/ mixed peel

¾ cup/115g apple, peeled, cored and roughly grated

3 extra-large (US)/large (UK) eggs, beaten

²/₃ cup/140ml brandy

butter, for greasing

You will need a 2½-pint/1.5-litre pudding basin

Prepare the beef-kidney suet by stripping out the membrane and colored spots, then grate on the coarse side of your grater, ending up with 1²/₃ cups/170g.

Sift the flour and salt together, then mix with the remaining dry ingredients, the dried fruit, the candied/mixed peel, the grated apple, and the suet.

Beat the eggs and brandy together, then stir the mixture into the dry ingredients. Mix it hard with a wooden spoon; make a wish as you do so.

Grease your pudding basin and line the bottom with a circle of baking parchment paper. Pack the mixture into the basin. Cover with a square of parchment paper or greased greaseproof paper and a pudding cloth or piece of kitchen foil on top; make a pleat in both layers to allow room for expansion during cooking. Tie very tightly with string.

Place the basin in a large pan and pour in enough boiling water to come about halfway up the basin; cover with a lid and steam or boil for 3½ hours, adding more boiling water to the pan as necessary so it doesn't boil dry.

When cooked, remove the paper and cloth or foil from the top of the basin and replace with fresh paper. Keep in a cool, dry place until required.

When ready to eat, steam or boil again for 1½–2 hours. Serve with Punch Sauce (see page 109).

THE AUTHOR'S CHRISTMAS PUDDING

To three ounces of flour, and the same weight of fine, lightly-grated bread-crumbs, add six of beef kidney-suet, chopped small, six of raisins weighed after they are stoned, six of well-cleaned currants, four ounces of minced apples, five of sugar, two of candied orange-rind, half a teaspoonful of nutmeg mixed with pounded mace, a very little salt, a small glass of brandy, and three whole eggs. Mix and beat these ingredients well together, tie them tightly in a thickly-floured cloth, and boil them for three hours and a half. We can recommend this as a remarkable light small rich pudding; it may be served with German wine, or punch sauce.

Flour, 3 oz; bread-crumbs, 3 oz; suet, stoned raisins, and currants, each 6 oz; minced apples, 4 oz; sugar, 5 oz; candied peel, 2 oz; spice, ½ teaspoonful; salt, few grains; brandy, small wineglassful; eggs, 3: 3½ hours.

ELIZA ACTON, *Modern Cookery for Private Families*, 1845

~ PUNCH SAUCE ~

Eliza Acton suggests serving her pudding with German wine or punch sauce. This is an intoxicating recipe, guaranteed to keep out the cold and, according to Bob Sawyer in *The Pickwick Papers*, to ward off rheumatism; "if ever hot punch did fail to act as a preventive, it was merely because the patient fell into the vulgar error of not taking enough of it."

1 lemon

2 oranges

¼ cup/50g light brown muscovado sugar

¾ cup/175ml sweet white wine

2 tablespoons rum

2 tablespoons brandy

3 tablespoons/40g unsalted butter

2 teaspoons all-purpose/plain flour

Pare the zest in strips from half the lemon and half an orange, taking care that you don't get any of the bitter white pith. Squeeze the juice from both oranges and from half the lemon. Put the strips of zest in a pan with the sugar and ⅓ cup/150ml water. Simmer them gently for 15–20 minutes, then remove and discard the zest.

Add the juices, the wine, rum, and brandy and heat gently but do not allow it to boil.

Blend the butter and flour together until you have a smooth paste. Add this, about a teaspoonful at a time, to the liquid, whisking well after each addition. As the butter melts into the sauce, the flour will thicken it.

Keep the sauce hot, but below boiling point, and serve in a warm pitcher/jug.

PUNCH SAUCE FOR SWEET PUDDINGS

This may be served with custard, plain bread, and plum-puddings. With two ounces of sugar and a quarter of a pint of water, boil very gently the rind of half a small lemon, and somewhat less of orange-peel, from fifteen to twenty minutes; strain out the rinds, thicken the sauce with an ounce and a half of butter and nearly a teaspoonful of flour, add a half-glass of brandy, the same of white wine, two-thirds of a glass of rum, with the juice of half an orange, and rather less of lemon-juice; serve the sauce very hot, but do not allow it to boil after the spirit is stirred in.

Sugar, 20 oz; water, ¼ pint; lemon and orange-rind; 14 to 20 minutes. Butter, 1½ oz; flour, 1 teaspoonful; brandy and white wine, each ½ wineglassful; rum, two-thirds of glassful; orange and lemon-juice.

ELIZA ACTON, *Modern Cookery for Private Families*, 1845

❦ FRENCH PLUMS ❦

The French Plums that Scrooge sees in the greengrocer's are "blushed in modest tartness from their highly-decorated boxes" (which, if "exceedingly ornamental," even Mrs. Beeton concedes might be put directly on the dining table). Port and cinnamon turn too-tart plums into a Christmas delight. Candied French plums were Christmas gifts, but should not be confused with "sugar plums," which are, in fact, sugared nuts or seeds.

SERVES 4

3 tablespoons water or juice of 1 orange

3 tablespoons port

1 tablespoon soft brown sugar

a cinnamon stick

a small piece of orange or lemon rind

approx. 1 lb 2 oz/500g French plums, halved and stones removed

Put the water or orange juice, port, sugar, cinnamon stick, and lemon rind in a pan and heat gently until the sugar has dissolved and you have a syrup.

Add the plums, cover, and stew gently for 15 minutes.

Serve with cream, Italian Cream (see page 157), or custard. Alternatively, make into a plum pie by mixing the ingredients together in a pie dish, adding a pastry lid (see pastry recipe on page 129), and baking at 400°F/200°C/Gas 6 for 30–35 minutes.

STEWED PLUMS

Put twelve French plums in a stew-pan, with a spoonful of brown sugar, a gill of water, a little cinnamon, and some thin rind of a lemon; let them stew twenty minutes, then pour them in a basin until cold, take them from their syrup and eat them dry. They are some-times stewed in wine and water, either port, sherry, or claret.

ALEXIS SOYER, *The Modern Housewife or Ménagère*, 1849

SHOPPING FOR FOOD

Dickens' involvement in his domestic affairs intrigued society—a party guest gossiped to Nathaniel Hawthorne (who related it in his *English Notebooks*) about Dickens "making bargains at butchers and bakers, and doing, as far as he could, whatever duty pertains to an English wife." He wrote to Catherine on May 5, 1856, anticipating a party he was planning while she and the family were in Paris, about buying "cold viands from Fortnum and Mason's." His household accounts show him spending far more than his wife, and he loved to be surrounded by fine things. It is easy to imagine the 12-year-old Dickens, like David Copperfield, tormenting himself by gazing at the luxuries he aspired to, window-shopping for venison in London's Fleet Street and pineapples at Covent Garden Market, but spending his pennies, when he had them, on a slice of bread and butter and some ready-made coffee from a street stall.

Almost any cheap food could be bought in the streets from a range of street-traders, known as costermongers. Dickens' friend, the journalist and campaigner, Henry Mayhew, interviewed hundreds of men, women, and children, to describe to his middle-class readers what it was like to eke out a living, buying wares—fruit, pet-meat, oysters, eels—from the markets at around 5am to sell on the streets over a long and ill-nourished day. Everybody specialized—Mayhew found sellers of watercress, hot elder wine, ham sandwiches, and curds and whey. Fried fish was increasingly popular, especially with Irish and other Catholic immigrants, who ate it on "fast" days. The "baked potatoe" men (whose wares were used as handwarmers as well as food), the coffee-stall, and the muffin man all competed for custom; the exploitative businessman, Ralph Nickleby, plans to put the muffin-sellers out of business with the "United Metropolitan Improved Hot Muffin and Crumpet Baking and Punctual Delivery Company."

Besides these barrows and street-trays, shops were caverns of luxury. The ghost of Christmas Present takes Scrooge window-shopping, and they marvel at piles of figs, chestnuts, filberts, Norfolk biffins, candied fruit, French plums in decorated boxes... everything "that was good to eat and in its Christmas dress." Shops were not for the poor; Maggy, in *Little Dorrit*, gazes at the tea caddies in the grocer's window, picking out the letters to practice her reading; the small servant in

By the 1840s, licensed dealers in game such as this one were able to sell what was once the preserve of the landed gentry.

The Old Curiosity Shop unpacking a hamper of treasures "had never thought it possible that such things could be, except in shops."

There were separate poulterers for birds and butchers for meat (mostly mutton, but also pork and, the pride of gastronomic England, beef). Steaks were wrapped in cabbage leaves to be carried home—Tom Pinch's butcher sees him pocketing his awkwardly and begs to do it for him, "'for meat,' he said, with some emotion, 'must be humoured, not drove'.." The better-off bought their food on credit and had it delivered to the house.

Catherine's menus are thoughtfully devised according to what was in season and available (see pages 30–31). By the time she published, the rail network was bringing fish and seafood, including the couple's beloved Yarmouth bloaters, from the east coast into London; meat could also be brought fresh to the city, avoiding the cruelty of the livestock market at Smithfield that Dickens abhorred (see pages 134–35). Fresh milk from the countryside surrounding London slowly replaced that from the urban dairies, such as the one where Mr. Wilfer buys the milk and cottage loaf for the celebratory tea in *Our Mutual Friend*. Until 1831, game such as venison, pheasant, or hare couldn't legally be sold, reserving it for those who had their own land on which to shoot or hunt. Dickens' letters show that he appreciated venison and a gift of wild duck the family had for Christmas. A hare hanging in Mrs. Joe's larder frightens the life out of Pip, in *Great Expectations*; country people had more access to game and rabbit (not necessarily through legal channels), but it is seldom part of the diet of Dickens' urban or working-class characters.

~ LEICESTERSHIRE PORK PIE ~

In *Great Expectations*, Pip's stolen pork pie would have been made to
a Kentish recipe, but the finest came from the town of Melton Mowbray in
Leicestershire, traditionally eaten by hunting folk in the eighteenth century.
The pies were raised by hand, made with fresh pork, a tiny drop of anchovy
essence to help flavor the meat, and jellied stock. In his recipe of 1846,
Francatelli omits the anchovy and the stock, but Dorothy Hartley's
Food in England (published in 1954) reinstates them.

MAKES 6

For the pork jelly

2 lb 3 oz/1kg pork bones

2 pig's trotters (ask your butcher
to split them)

1 onion, roughly chopped

2 carrots, roughly chopped

1 bouquet garni (or a truss of sage
and marjoram)

some apple cores (the pips add
a slightly almond flavor and
a little acid)

or, instead of all the above
ingredients, 3 gelatine leaves and
1¼ cups/300ml well-flavored
stock

For the filling

approx. 1 lb 9 oz/700g boned
shoulder of pork (keep the bone
for the stock)

approx. 2 oz/50g belly of pork

approx. 2 oz/50g unsmoked
bacon

3 sage leaves, very finely chopped

1 teaspoon thyme or marjoram
leaves, very finely chopped

1 teaspoon anchovy essence

¼ teaspoon grated nutmeg or
ground mace

salt and freshly ground white
pepper

For the pastry

¾ cup plus 2 tablespoons/200g
lard

1 cup/220ml water or milk,
or a mix of half and half

4 cups/575g strong all-purpose/
plain white flour

1 teaspoon salt

1 egg, beaten, to glaze

You will need a wooden pie dolly
or a jam jar

If making your own jelly, put the pork jelly ingredients in a stockpot
with 2–3 quarts/2–3 litres of water. Just cover with water, bring to
the boil, and simmer, partially covered, for about 4 hours. Skim off
any scum from the surface from time to time. Let it cool a little and
strain it through a strainer/sieve.

Reduce the stock to about 1¼ cups/300ml by leaving it on a rolling
boil in an uncovered pan—the wider the pan, the better.

Prepare the filling. Chop the pork shoulder into cubes about ½ inch/
1cm square or smaller (a meat cleaver is useful for this). Mince or
finely chop the pork belly and bacon. Mix these up well with the rest
of the filling ingredients. If you aren't sure about the seasoning, fry a

little piece in hot oil to taste. You can do this the night before and leave in the fridge to let the flavors develop.

Preheat the oven to 350°F/180°C/Gas 4. Grease a baking tray.

For the pastry, put the lard into a pan with the liquid and heat gently until it is melted and the liquid is hot but not boiling. Sift the flour and salt into a large bowl and make a well in the center. Pour the hot liquid into the well and beat with a wooden spoon until it is well mixed, then knead well until smooth.

Divide the pastry into six equal parts. For each part, pinch off a quarter for the pie lid and roll out the remainder to about ¾ inch/2cm thick. Cover a pie dolly or jam jar in plastic wrap/clingfilm and flour it well; invert it and drape the pastry over, pressing it down the sides until it is about 2–2½ inches/5–6cm high. Cut a clean top edge with a knife.

Upturn the jar and carefully ease the dolly or jar and plastic wrap/clingfilm out of the pastry. Pack a sixth of the meat mixture into the pastry, pressing it down so there are no air gaps.

Roll out the top pastry and cut it to the same size as the pie; punch out a small round hole in the center for the air to escape (and the jelly to go in). Place it on top of the meat, inside the edges of the pastry case, and pinch the sides and top together with wet fingers. You can make it more upright by pushing it gently with your cupped hands and turning it, as if it were a pot on a potter's wheel.

Decorate the top of the pie with scraps of pastry. Dorothy Hartley says "Pie art has moved with the times, and the most modern pies have now an austerity of outline. Nevertheless, an acorn or a rosette is suitable, and four oak leaves or a beech-nut in paste show a nice feeling for the pig's previous environment." Brush with the beaten egg. Repeat to make the remaining pies.

Carefully transfer the pies to the greased baking tray. Bake in the preheated oven for about 1 hour 20 minutes, but check them after an hour. If they are browning too quickly, cover with baking parchment paper.

Leave the pies to cool. The filling contracts as they cool, leaving gaps for the jelly to fill.

If you are making jelly from gelatine, soak the leaves in cold water for 10 minutes, then squeeze out the excess water and dissolve the gelatine in the warm stock.

Make sure your stock is just about liquid—somewhere between tepid and warm. Using a funnel, pour it through the hole in the top of each pie. Leave to set overnight in a cool place or in the fridge.

LEICESTERSHIRE PORK PIE

Cut the pork up in square pieces, fat and lean, about the size of a cob-nut, season with pepper and salt, and a small quantity of sage and thyme chopped fine, and set it aside on a dish in a cool place. Next, make some hot-water-paste, using for this purpose (if desired) fresh-made hog's lard instead of butter, in the proportion of eight ounces to the pound of flour. These pies must be raised by hand, in the following manner:-

First mould the paste into a round ball upon the slab, then roll it out to the thickness of half an inch, and with the back of the right hand indent the centre in a circle reaching to within three inches of the edge of the paste; next, gather up the edges all round, pressing it closely with the fingers and thumbs, so as to give to it the form of a purse; then continue to work it upwards, until the sides are raised sufficiently high; the pie should now be placed on a baking-sheet, with a round of buttered paper under it, and after it has been filled with the pork – previously prepared for this purpose, covered in with some of the paste in the usual manner. Trim the edges and pinch it round with the pincers, decorate it, egg it over and bake it until done: calculating the time it should remain in the oven, according to the quantity of meat it contains.

CHARLES ELME FRANCATELLI, *The Modern Cook*, 1846

~ PICKLED PORK ~

Pork legs, such as the one that Pip's ferocious sister serves at their Christmas dinner, were often pickled with dry salt which enabled them to keep for many months. Hannah Glasse's recipe for a wet cure is easier to do and could be used in two ways. Season roast pork by leaving the leg in the pickle overnight, before drying and roasting as usual. Alternatively, pickle it for about a week to make a beautiful Christmas ham that can be braised and then eaten hot or cold.

SERVES 12–16

1 half leg of pork (weighing about 6½ lb/3kg)

For the pickle

5 pints/3 litres water (substitute 1 quart/1 litre with hard/strong cider or ale if you wish)

14 oz/400g curing salt (i.e. salt with the right proportion of sodium nitrite, which keeps it pink)

1¾ cups/350g dark soft brown sugar or molasses/black treacle

plus any of the following optional flavorings:

a small bunch of thyme

3 sprigs of rosemary

4 bay leaves

2 tablespoons juniper berries or allspice berries, slightly crushed

a fragment of nutmeg

2 teaspoons cloves

2 teaspoons black peppercorns, slightly crushed

To boil the pickled pork

stock vegetables, such as 1 large peeled onion, 2 roughly chopped carrots, and 2 roughly chopped parsnips

2 bay leaves

a small bunch of parsley stalks

a small bunch of chives

a sprig of thyme

a sprig of marjoram

10 peppercorns

For the glaze

2 tablespoons honey or soft brown sugar

1 tablespoon English or French mustard, or to taste

1½ cups/50g day-old breadcrumbs

To make the pickle, bring the water, cider or ale (if using), salt, and sugar or molasses/treacle to the boil in a non-corrosive saucepan (stainless steel is fine); make sure it doesn't boil over. Skim the scum from the surface, then add the herbs and spices, making sure the salt and sugar dissolve. Let the pickling brine cool completely. When cold, you can check that it's salty enough by floating a fresh egg on the surface!

Put the pork in a large, non-metallic container, such as a bowl or food-grade bucket. Strain the brine over, making sure it covers the meat; you could weigh down the meat with a plastic weight or some upturned soup bowls. Cover and refrigerate or store at 43–46°F/6–8°C.

Either take the pork out of the brine the following day, rinse, and let it dry before roasting as normal, or leave it soaking in the brine for 5–7 days. Check the brine every day—if it begins to smell off, discard it, and cover the meat with fresh brine.

The day before you want to cook the pork, remove it from the brine, rinse, and dry with kitchen paper. Hang the pork in a cold, dry, airy place if you can for 24 hours. If not, wrap it in a clean cotton cloth and keep in the fridge.

To boil the pork, place it in a large pan of cold water and bring it to the boil; if the water tastes salty, discard it, replace with fresh cold water, and repeat until the cooking water tastes only lightly salted. Then add the stock vegetables, herbs, and seasonings to the pan and simmer the meat very gently for 22–27 minutes per 1 lb or 25–30 minutes per 500g. Skim any scum from the surface. Remove from the heat and leave the meat to cool in the cooking liquid for 15–20 minutes.

Preheat the oven to 400°F/200°C/Gas 6.

Peel away the skin from the meat, leaving the fat, and place the meat in a large roasting pan. Score the fat in a diamond pattern, mix the honey or sugar and mustard together, spread this glaze evenly over, and cover with the breadcrumbs. Bake in the preheated oven for 15–20 minutes to crisp the breadcrumbs. Cover and let it stand for 15–20 minutes before carving, or eat cold.

A PICKLE FOR PORK, WHICH IS TO BE EAT SOON

You must take two Gallons of Pump-water, one Pound of Bay-salt, one Pound of coarse Sugar, six Ounces of Salt-petre, boil it all together, and skim it when cold. Cut the Pork in what Pieces you please, lay it down close, and pour the Liquor over it. Lay a Weight on it to keep it close, and cover it close from the Air, and it will be fit to use in a Week. If you find the Pickle begins to spoil, boil the Pickle again, and skim it; when it is cold, pour it on your Pork again.

HANNAH GLASSE, *The Art of Cookery Made Plain and Easy,* 1747

TO DRESS A HAM A LA BRAISE

Clear the Knuckle, take off the Swerd, and lay it in Water to freshen; then tye it about with a String, take Slices of Bacon and Beef, beat and season them well with Spice and Sweet Herbs; then lay them in the Bottom of a Kettle with Onions, Parsnips, and Carrots sliced, with some Cives [sic] and Parsley; Lay in your Ham the Fat Side uppermost, and cover it with Slices of Beef, and over that Slices of Bacon; then lay on some sliced Roots and Herbs, the same as under it; Cover it close, and stop it close with Paste, put Fire both over and under it, and let it stew with a very slow Fire twelve Hours; put it in a Pan, drudge it well with grated Bread, and brown it with a hot Iron; then serve it up on a clean Napkin, garnished with raw Parsley.

HANNAH GLASSE, *The Art of Cookery Made Plain and Easy,* 1747

~ CHESTNUT AND APPLE MINCE PIES ~

This old Scottish recipe brings together the chestnuts from the trees around
Joe's forge and the mincemeat that went into Mrs. Joe's "handsome mince-
pie," made before Pip stole the leftovers for Magwitch. The Cratchit family
also enjoy the tradition of roasting chestnuts on the fire at Christmas, but
the English have never got into the habit of cooking with them. The chestnut
paste lightens the mix and gives a delightful toffee-ish taste.

MAKES 12 DEEP-FILLED PIES

1 lb 2oz/500g shortcrust
pastry, or shortcrust pastry
made with 2⅔ cups/350g
all-purpose/plain flour,
¾ cup/175g fat, and 1 egg
yolk (see recipe on page 129)

beaten egg or milk, to glaze

For the mincemeat

1 large cooking apple,
peeled, cored, and finely
chopped (approx. 7 oz/
200g)

1 cup/200g cooked
chestnuts, finely chopped

6½ tablespoons/80g dark
soft brown sugar

1 teaspoon ground
cinnamon

2 tablespoons brandy

zest of an orange or
clementine

1½ cups/180g mixed raisins,
currants, and golden
raisins/sultanas

½ cup/60g candied/mixed
peel

1 cup/100g suet

To make the mincemeat, cook the apple, chestnuts, and sugar together
in a very little water for 15–20 minutes until soft and toffee-ish. Purée
them together with the cinnamon, brandy, and orange zest. Adjust the
flavorings to taste. Mix in the dried fruit and suet. (If you are keeping
your mincemeat, let the mixture cool before adding the suet, so it
doesn't melt.)

Preheat the oven to 400°F/200°C/Gas 6.

Roll out the pastry to about ⅛ inch/3mm thick, and cut into rounds
of about 4 inches/10cm to line muffin trays. Fill each pastry case with
mincemeat, packing down the mixture.

Roll out the remaining pastry and cut into rounds of about 3¼ inches/
8cm to form the lids. Crimp them together and seal with beaten egg or
milk. Decorate the tops (or replace the lids) with holly leaves, stars,
angels, or bells, cut from the pastry trimmings, then brush the surface
with beaten egg or milk.

Bake in the preheated oven for about 15–20 minutes until the pastry
is golden.

FOR A CHESTNUT FLORENTIN

*Take your apples and peel them and take out the hearts, then take and boil
your chestnuts till the skins come of and some orange peel & sedron and cut
in small pieces, & synemon, & resons, & white whine & for a peast take a
pound of butter and a forpet of flour, and roll it out and some shuggar...*

Anonymous Scottish Cookbook Manuscript,

NATIONAL LIBRARY OF SCOTLAND

[forpet = fourth of a peck; sedron = candied citron; peast = paste/pastry]

TWELFTH CAKE

Charles and Catherine's first son, Charley, was born on Twelfth Night (January 6) and every year his godmother, Angela Burdett-Coutts, would send a huge Twelfth Cake for his birthday. One cake followed the Dickens family to Genoa, where a Swiss pastry cook repaired a chip in its highly decorative frosting and displayed it in his window for the townsfolk to admire. In 1870 Queen Victoria, believing it was too rowdy, had the feast of Twelfth Night removed from the holiday calendar, and the cake migrated to Christmas.

SERVES ABOUT 20

3 cups/400g all-purpose/plain flour

1 teaspoon grated nutmeg

½ teaspoon ground cinnamon

¼ teaspoon ground allspice

¼ teaspoon ground mace

¼ teaspoon ground ginger

¼ teaspoon ground coriander

a pinch of salt

1½ cups plus 2 teaspoons/350g butter, softened, plus extra for greasing

1¾ cups/350g soft brown sugar or golden granulated/caster sugar

grated zest of ½ lemon

6 US extra large/UK large free-range eggs, beaten

2 tablespoons brandy

7½ cups/1kg currants (or 4½ cups/600g currants and 1½ cups/200g each raisins and golden raisins/sultanas)

1½ cups/200g cut candied/mixed peel (or ¾ cup/100g peel and ¾ cup/100g candied citron, if you can find it)

1 cup/100g almonds, chopped or flaked

For the almond paste

4½ cups/450g ground almonds

3 cups/350g confectioners'/icing sugar, sifted

approx. 2 tablespoons liquid, such as orange or lemon juice, orange-flower water, brandy, or liqueur

or, instead of the separate ingredients, 1¾ lb/800g store-bought white almond paste/marzipan

For the frosting

2 lb/900g royal icing sugar

7 tablespoons water

blue food coloring

white fondant decorations

You will need a deep round cake pan/tin 9 inches/23cm in diameter, plus molds for the decorations. Also, for the sake of tradition, a ceramic bean and a ceramic pea

Preheat the oven to 300°F/150°C/Gas 2. Grease and line the cake pan/tin, using a double thickness of greaseproof paper.

Sift the flour and spices into a large bowl with a pinch of salt.

Put the softened butter, sugar, and lemon zest into a bowl and beat together until pale and fluffy. Add the beaten eggs a very little at a time; sprinkle in a spoonful of the flour if the mixture begins to separate. Beat in the brandy. Fold in the flour using a metal spoon, followed by the fruit, peel, and nuts.

To make it a proper Twelfth Cake, hide a ceramic bean and pea in the mixture. Whoever finds them in their slice becomes the King and Queen (respectively) of the Twelfth Night celebrations.

Spoon the mixture into the prepared cake pan/tin and bake in the preheated oven for 2½ hours. Cover the top of the cake with paper if it is browning too quickly. Turn the oven down to 275°F/140°C/Gas 1 for a further 1½ hours. Check the cake after it has been in the oven for 3½ hours—it is done when a skewer inserted into the middle comes out clean. Let the cake cool a little and then turn it out of the pan and cool on a wire rack.

To make your own almond paste, mix the ground almonds in a bowl with the sifted confectioners'/icing sugar; add the liquid little by little and mix well until you have a pliable dough that isn't too sticky to roll out.

To cover the cold cake with almond paste or marzipan, roll it out to ⅛–¼ inch/3–5mm thick. Using your cake pan/tin as a guide, cut out a circle for the top. Cut three lengths of 9½ inches/24cm for the sides. Place on and around the cake, then smooth the joins together with warm water. Let the almond paste dry.

For the frosting, sift the sugar into the bowl of an electric mixer, sprinkle the water over the top, and beat slowly at first, to avoid clouds of sugar. When it is combined, add blue coloring drop by drop and continue to beat until it is the desired mid-blue color.

Ice the cake with two coats of blue royal icing, letting the first one dry overnight. Decorate with white fondant icing decorations, such as fleur de lys and crowns on top for the king and queen.

TWELFTH CAKE

Two pounds of sifted flour, two pounds of sifted loaf sugar, two pounds of butter, eighteen eggs, four pounds of currants, one half pound of almonds blanched and chopped, one half pound of citron, one pound of candied orange and lemon-peel cut into thin slices, a large nutmeg grated, half an ounce of ground allspice; ground cinnamon, mace, ginger, and corianders, a quarter of an ounce of each, and a gill of brandy.

Put the butter into a stew-pan, in a warm place, and work it into a smooth cream with the hand, and mix it with the sugar and spice in a pan (or on your paste board) for some time; then break in the eggs by degrees, and beat it at least twenty minutes; stir in the brandy, and then the flour, and work it a little; add the fruit, sweetmeats, and almonds, and mix all together lightly; have ready a hoop cased with paper, on a baking-plate; put in the mixture, smooth it on the top with your hand, dipped in milk; put the plate on another, with sawdust between, to prevent the bottom from colouring too much: bake it in a slow oven four hours or more, and when nearly cold, ice it with Icing for Twelfth or Bride Cake.

ICING FOR TWELFTH OR BRIDE CAKE

Take one pound of double-refined sugar, pounded and sifted through a lawn sieve; put into a pan quite free from grease; break in the whites of six eggs, and as much powder blue as will lie on a sixpence; beat it well with a spattle for ten minutes; then squeeze in the juice of a lemon, and beat it till it becomes thick and transparent. Set the cake you intend to ice in an oven or warm place five minutes; then spread over the top and sides with the mixture as smooth as possible. If for a wedding-cake only, plain ice it; if for a twelfth cake, ornament it with gum paste, or fancy articles of any description.

Obs. -A good twelfth cake, not baked too much, and kept in a cool dry place, will retain its moisture and eat well, if twelve months old.

WILLIAM KITCHINER, *Apicius Redivivus, or The Cook's Oracle*, 1817

CHAPTER 8

Food for the Poor

Oliver Twist *and* A Tale of Two Cities

◆

Oliver Asks for More
George Cruikshank

Every Dickens reader associates gruel with Oliver Twist's pathetic request for more, and it is easy to think that gruel was an affliction imposed only on the workhouse poor; however, it was a staple cooked in homes too. In *Household Words*, Dickens (writing with William Wills) complains that the poor would rather eat gruel or slowly starve than eat fish. Queen Victoria's chef, Charles Elmé Francatelli, offers five recipes for gruel in *A Plain Cookery Book for the Working Classes*. Alexis Soyer and other celebrity chefs also wrote cookbooks for the poor, or for the people who ran soup kitchens or institutions that attempted to feed them, particularly as the Europe-wide potato blight that devastated Ireland meant a generation of poor in the 1840s had to learn new ways of eating and cooking.

Dickens deliberately balanced descriptions of starving children with the greed or selfishness of the well-fed adults who were supposed to care for them. Mr. Bumble, the board, and the master of the workhouse in *Oliver Twist* are all simply described as "fat," while Oliver Twist and the workhouse boys "suffered the tortures of slow starvation." Dickens knew his middle-class readers would readily pity women and children but would fear the hunger of grown men such as Magwitch, associated as it was with criminality and rioting. The seething description of hunger in *A Tale of Two Cities* shows how lack of food could lead to rage, desperation, and (most worryingly of all) revolution: "Hunger stared down from the smokeless chimneys, and started up from the filthy street that had no offal, among its refuse, of anything to eat. Hunger was the inscription on the baker's shelves, written in every small loaf of his scanty stock of bad bread; at the sausage-shop, in every dead-dog preparation that was offered for sale."

Sam Weller, who could see the funny side even of poverty, tells Mr. Pickwick that it always seems to go with oysters, which in Victorian times were plentiful and cheap: "Blessed if I don't think that ven a man's wery poor, he rushes out of his lodgings, and eats oysters in reg'lar desperation."

~ GRUEL ~

A *Plain Cookery Book for the Working Classes* is not for the impoverished; Francatelli expects his readers to save up for an oven and put brandy or other spirits, butter, and cinnamon in their gruel. Standard gruel was made from grits, or groats (meaning whole, husked oats); he offers varieties for oatmeal (rolled and steamed oats), rice, pearl barley, and Indian corn (known as Brown and Polson).

SERVES 4

¾ cup/90g groats (available in wholefood stores) or unrefined oatmeal

3 cups/700ml water

a pinch of salt (optional)

butter (optional)

This makes a thick, nutritious oatmeal/porridge, a little like a risotto (unlike Victorian gruel which could be quite thin). Serve with brown sugar and butter; fresh fruit or fruit compôte; cream or milk; or whisky.

Soak the groats in the water overnight.

Add a pinch of salt, if using, and simmer, partially covered, over a low heat, for up to an hour, until all the water is absorbed and the mixture is thick and soft (oatmeal will take less time than groats). Alternatively, butter a slow cooker and leave on low overnight or for 7–8 hours.

HOW TO MAKE GRUEL

Mix a table-spoonful of Robinson's prepared groats or grits with a tea-cupful of cold water, pour this into a saucepan containing a pint of hot water, and stir it on the fire while it boils for ten minutes; strain the gruel through a sieve or colander into a basin, sweeten to taste, add a spoonful of any kind of spirits, or else season the gruel with salt and a bit of butter.

CHARLES ELME FRANCATELLI, *A Plain Cookery Book for the Working Classes*, 1852

RABBIT PIE

Thanks to poachers, rabbit meat made a rare feast of protein for the rural poor; in the twentieth century's times of hardship, many bunny-loving children were told they were eating "chicken." In *Oliver Twist*, when a convalescent Bill Sikes is holed up, Fagin, the Artful Dodger, and Charley Bates bring him "Sitch a rabbit pie, Bill... sitch delicate creeturs, with sitch tender limbs, Bill, that the wery bones melt in your mouth."

SERVES 4–6

approx. 2 lb 3 oz/1kg wild rabbit, jointed, or approx. 1 lb 9 oz/700g rabbit meat

all-purpose/plain flour, for dusting, well-seasoned with salt, freshly ground black pepper, and a little nutmeg

olive oil, for frying

4½ oz/125g slices of streaky bacon, diced

2 onions, finely chopped

5½ oz/150g button mushrooms, halved or quartered

2 teaspoons freshly chopped thyme

1 bay leaf

2 cups plus 2 tablespoons/500ml light stock, such as chicken or vegetable

2–3 carrots, chopped

2 tablespoons freshly chopped parsley

For the pastry

1¾ cups/225g all-purpose/plain flour

a pinch of salt

½ cup/110g very cold butter

iced water

1 egg yolk

a little beaten egg, to glaze

To make the pastry, sift the flour and salt into a large bowl. Cut the cold butter into the flour using a knife, making the pieces as small as possible, then stir until every piece is coated with flour. Using your fingertips, rub the fat into the flour until it is no longer visible. Add 2 tablespoons iced water to the egg yolk, and stir this into the flour. Mix with the blade of a knife, adding a little more cold water to make it into a stiff paste. Bring it together with your hands, touching it as little as possible. Form into a ball, cover with plastic wrap/clingfilm, and chill in the fridge for 20–30 minutes or until ready to use.

Roll the rabbit joints or meat in the seasoned flour. Warm the olive oil in a wide pan, add the meat in batches and brown on both sides, removing the meat to one side as each batch is browned.

Add the bacon to the pan and fry until the fat begins to run, then add the onion to the oil and sweat slowly until it begins to soften. Add the mushrooms and fry until they begin to soften.

Return the rabbit to the bacon and vegetable mixture in the pan, with the thyme and bay leaf. Add the stock and if necessary enough water to just cover the meat. Scrape the bottom of the pan to release all the sticky, fried bits. Add extra seasoning to taste. Bring it to a simmer, partially covered. Cook rabbit on the bone for about 1 hour; rabbit pieces for about 45 minutes. Add the carrots 30 minutes before the end of the cooking time.

Remove the cooked rabbit pieces from the pan, then pick out the bones with your hands and discard them. Discard the bay leaf.

You should have a stew with a good thick gravy. If you need to reduce the gravy, strain everything through a strainer/sieve, put the meat and vegetables into a greased 2½-pint/1.5-litre baking dish, then boil the gravy down until you have about 1 cup/250ml. If you need to thicken your gravy, mix a dessertspoon of all-purpose/plain flour with a dessertspoon of butter. Add pea-sized amounts of this beurre manié to the pan until you have the required thickness. Add the chopped parsley to the gravy, then pour it over the meat and vegetables in the baking dish.

Preheat the oven to gas 400°F/200°C/Gas 6.

Roll the pastry out to 2 inches/5cm wider than the top of your baking dish. Cut a 2-inch/5-cm strip and put this around the top of the dish, wet the top of it, and sit the pastry circle on top. Crimp the edges of the pastry together. Decorate the top of the pie with pastry trimmings and glaze with beaten egg. Make a hole in the center of the pastry to let the steam escape. Bake for 25–30 minutes, until the pastry is golden brown.

RABBIT PIE

Cut the rabbit up as for pudding; roll the pieces in flour, then put them in the pie-dish, with some slices of ham or bacon; season with salt, pepper, chopped onions, nutmeg, (grated, if handy), according to size; add half-a-pint of water; cover, and bake.
A teaspoonful of curry may be added, instead of pepper.

ALEXIS SOYER, *A Shilling Cookery for the People*, 1854

Pastry recipe adapted from "A Cold Crust,"
HANNAH GLASSE, *The Art of Cookery Made Plain and Easy*, 1747

CHARITABLE SOUP

Catherine Dickens' menu book is most indebted to the recipes of the celebrity chef Alexis Soyer. In 1847, in the midst of the Irish potato famine, he traveled to Dublin to set up a famine-relief kitchen and wrote *Soyer's Charitable Cookery*, the proceeds of which he gave to charity. He later traveled to the Crimea to change the diet of soldiers, particularly those in hospital.

SERVES 6

2 onions, sliced

a little olive oil, for frying

2 leeks, sliced and washed free of grit

2 sticks of celery, chopped

2 lb 3 oz/1kg shin of beef or neck of lamb, bone in, cut into pieces by your butcher, plus some stock bones

2 small turnips, chopped

bouquet garni or 2 bay leaves and a few sprigs of thyme and curly parsley, tied together

8½ cups/2 litres water (or beef stock if you are using meat without bones)

6 tablespoons pearl barley

3 carrots, chopped

salt and freshly ground black pepper

Preheat the oven, if using, to 325°F/165°C/Gas 3.

Sauté the onions in a little olive oil in a skillet/frying pan until they begin to soften, then add the leeks and celery and continue to soften for 5 minutes.

Tip this into a saucepan. Add a little more oil to the pan and brown the meat lightly on all sides in two batches—don't let it sweat in the pan—then add it to the onions. Add the turnips, herbs, and either stock or cold water plus the stock bones. Season with salt and pepper, bring to a simmer and simmer on a very low heat, or cover and put it in the preheated oven, for 1½ hours.

Add the pearl barley and carrots and continue to simmer for 45 minutes, or until the pearl barley is cooked. Toward the end of the cooking time, take the stock bones and herbs out of the pan and discard.

Take the meat out of the broth, pull it off the bones and shred it, then return the meat to the pan.

CHARITABLE SOUP

Receipt no. 1 is a basic scotch broth for two gallons; he also scales it up for 100 gallons.
Prices are given in shillings (s) and old (pre-decimal) pennies (d).

	£	s	d
Twelve pounds of solid meat, at 4d per lb. cut into pieces one inch square, or sixteen pounds with bones at 3d per lb		4	0
Three pounds, two ounces of dripping		1	0
Twelve pounds of onions sliced thin		0	8
Six pounds of leeks (ditto)			
Six pounds of celery (ditto)		1	3
Eight pounds of turnips, washed only, and cut into dice half an inch square			
Thirty-seven pounds and a half of flour, seconds		7	0
Thirty-five pounds of pearl barley, previously soaked		6	9
Nine pounds of salt		0	3
One pound, seven ounces of sugar		0	9

£1 1s 8d

Have ready a spatula, or a piece of board the shape of a cricket bat, about six inches
wide, tapering towards the top as a handle, (which must be from one foot and a half
to two feet above the surface of the vessel), to stir with; take twelve pounds of solid meat,
or sixteen pounds with the bones, (legs or clods of beef is excellent for the purpose, but any
kind of edible meat from beef to doe venison will do), cut in pieces about one inch square;
put the dripping (if dripping cannot be had, use four pounds of fat) in the boiler – light
the fire – when the fat is melted, add the onions; fry ten minutes, stirring it all the time;
add the vegetables and the meat; fry for twenty minutes or until a thick glaze is produced;
then add the salt and sugar, and four gallons of cold water; then add the flour; keep
stirring quickly until quite smooth; add the barley, and fill by degrees with hot water;
boil for three hours, or until the barley is quite tender, and serve.

ALEXIS SOYER, *Charitable Cookery*, 1847

DICKENS THE SOCIAL CAMPAIGNER

The great, unspoken burden of Dickens' childhood was that his father was briefly incarcerated in the Marshalsea debtors' prison. At age 12, Dickens was humiliated by having to work in a blacking factory, rather than go to school with other boys of his age. These early experiences fuelled his first work as a Parliamentary Reporter, covering some of the most influential political changes in the early nineteenth century, including the infamous Poor Law Amendment Act of 1834. This outlawed charitable gifts of food, clothes, or money to the poor anywhere except in the workhouses, whose prison-like regimes were designed to repel all but the most desperate or the most hardened. Dickens' staggering portrayal of the workhouse in *Oliver Twist* was accurate—the child's plea for more gruel was answered by workhouse rules that forbade second helpings and recommended the sort of draconian punishments that Oliver was given.

Dickens hammers home to his readers the injustice of inequality by balancing scenes of enjoyable eating with images such as Jo, the London street-sweeper in *Bleak House*, breakfasting on a "dirty bit of bread" on the doorstep of the Society for the Propagation of the Gospel in Foreign Parts—a religious organization failing to help the needy, literally on their doorstep. He was part of a growing movement that entertained to inform. Benjamin Disraeli's novel, *Sybil: or the Two Nations* (1845) describes the rich and the poor as "two nations... fed by a different food."

Most of the food campaigning topics of the day found space in Dickens' magazine, *Household Words*. It amplified the findings of *The Lancet*, the medical journal which campaigned against the adulteration of food, after it found every one of 49 bread samples to be adulterated with at best inferior flour, at worst sulfate of lime and alum. Even after the Food Adulteration Acts of 1872 and 1875, the cookbook writer Theodore Garrett was warning readers against an alphabet of horrors, from the relatively benign, such as mustard husks in allspice, to the life-threatening sulfuric acid and lead in vinegar. Tea could be recycled tea leaves or any other leaves, or be adulterated with sand or iron. Henry Mayhew reported that out-of-date "Newcastle Pickled Salmon" was often flogged at public houses to the "Lushingtons" who, pickled themselves, wouldn't notice its taint. Meat could be anything. As Sam Weller

A workhouse warden (photographed in 1880) weighs out portions of bread for the unfortunate inmates. Even after Dickens' death, hunger was still an integral part of life in the workhouse.

says, unpacking a picnic: "Wery good thing is weal pie, when you know the lady as made it, and is quite sure it ain't kittens." In *Hard Times*, Bounderby, boasting of his deprived childhood, reckons he "had eaten in his youth at least three horses under the guise of polonies and saveloys" (types of sausage).

Dickens was appalled by the way livestock was treated and the corruption of dealers who sold the flesh of diseased animals. He wrote for *Household Words* on the cruelty, noise, goading, and filth of Britain's urban livestock markets. In the ironically titled *A Monument of French Folly*, he reported on the suburban slaughter houses in Paris and the more humane, quiet, orderly, and clean arrangements where the business was done with "Plenty of room; plenty of time."

Dickens also supported the right sort of direct action. His letters mention subscriptions he made to individuals and charities, such as a soup kitchen in Carlisle (to Henry Morley, December 19, 1861), and he poured energy into setting up Urania Cottage, a home for redeemed prostitutes. He believed that "Order and punctuality, cleanliness, the whole routine of household duties—as washing, mending, cooking" was the route to redemption for the women (letter to Angela Burdett-Coutts, May 26, 1846). Mealtimes were important, too—as he shows time and again in his novels, the enjoyment of good food is a social good in itself and a right, even of the poor and outcast in society.

BATTER PUDDING

The eight-year-old David Copperfield is (as usual) cheated by an unscrupulous waiter who exclaims that this is his favorite pudding, and helps himself with a tablespoon and a hearty appetite. Cooked with fresh fruit, batter pudding is a delight far different from the "stout pale pudding, heavy and flabby" with great flat raisins that the child turned to for ballast.

SERVES 6–8

14 oz/400g fruit, such as pitted/stoned cherries, pitted/stoned and quartered plums, blackberries with slices of apple, raspberries, gooseberries, or chopped rhubarb

½ cup/100g sugar (or more, depending on taste and the fruit used)

4 eggs

1⅓ cups/180g all-purpose/plain flour

1¼ cups/300ml milk

½ teaspoon vanilla extract (optional)

3½ tablespoons/50g butter, melted (optional), plus extra for greasing

Preheat the oven to 350°F/180°C/Gas 4. Butter a wide, flat pie dish of approx. 1¾-pint/1-litre capacity.

Tip the fruit into the dish. For sharp fruit such as gooseberries and rhubarb, mix the fruit with another another 5 teaspoons sugar.

Beat the sugar and eggs together, then sift in the flour, mixing it in well. Gradually add the milk and vanilla extract, if using. (For a richer pudding, heat the butter in a pan until just melted and stir it into the batter.)

Pour the batter over the fruit and bake in the preheated oven for 40–45 minutes. Serve hot with Pudding Sauce (see page 141).

A BATTER AND FRUIT PUDDING

Ingredients, two quarts of milk, one pound of flour, four eggs, eight ounces of sugar, one quart of fruit (either plums, gooseberries, currants, &c), one ounce of butter, a good pinch of salt. First, mix the flour, eggs, sugar, salt, and a pint of the milk, by working all together in a basin or pan, with a spoon, and when quite smooth, add the remainder of the milk; work the batter thoroughly, and pour it into a large pie-dish, greased with the butter; add the fruit, and bake the pudding for an hour and a quarter.

CHARLES ELME FRANCATELLI, *A Plain Cookery Book for the Working Classes*, 1852

ROLY-POLY JAM PUDDING

Frequently on Catherine's menus for smaller family parties when economy was more important than show, this was the best comfort food. Charles Kent, reminiscing about the dinner party that John Forster threw for what was to be Dickens' final birthday on February 7, 1870, wrote: "Forster had placed at Dickens's command that choicest sweet of his throughout his life from his earliest boyhood, a roly-poly jam pudding!" (reproduced in *The Dickensian*, Vol 89, 1993).

SERVES 6–8

butter, for greasing

1¾ cups/225g self-rising flour

½ level teaspoon salt

1 cup/100g shredded suet

approx. ⅔ cup/150ml cold water

approx. 6 level tablespoons dark jam (raspberry, strawberry, blackcurrant, or plum preserves all make a good contrast against the pale dough)

Cut a piece of baking parchment paper 10 x 14 inches/25 x 35cm. Grease with butter and place on a slightly larger piece of kitchen foil.

Mix the dry ingredients in a bowl. Add the water a little at a time, mixing with a knife to make a smooth, elastic dough.

Bring the dough together with your hands. Handling it as little as possible, roll it out to a rectangle (about ¼ inch/5mm deep and 8¾ x 10 inches/22 x 25cm, or narrower to fit the size of saucepan it will be steamed in).

Spread the jam all over the pastry, leaving ¾ inch/2cm clear around one short and two long edges (so the jam doesn't get squeezed out when it is rolled up). Brush milk or water onto the edges and loosely roll it up starting from the short, jammy edge.

Put it on the paper with the long seam underneath. Fold the paper and foil loosely around the pudding, giving it room to expand but tightly sealing the sides and end so the water does not get in.

Place the wrapped roll in a steamer or on a trivet or plate in a large saucepan of boiling water, cover, and steam for 1½–2 hours; check the water level every 30 minutes or so and top up if necessary.

Let the pudding rest for a minute or two before unwrapping. Serve in slices with Pudding Sauce (see page 141).

JAM PUDDING

Ingredients, one pound of flour, six ounces of suet, half-a-pint of water, a pinch of salt, one pound of any kind of common jam, at 7d. Mix the flour, suet, water and salt into a firm, compact kind of paste; roll this out with a rolling-pin, sprinkling some flour on the table to prevent the paste from sticking to either; fold up the paste, and roll it out again; repeat the rolling-out and folding three times; this operation will make the paste lighter. Next, roll out the paste one foot long by eighteen inches wide, spread the jam all over this, roll up the pudding in the form of a bolster, roll it up in a well-greased and floured cloth, tie it up tightly at both ends; put the pudding into a pot of boiling water, and boil it for nearly two hours; when done, turn out carefully on to its dish, without breaking the crust.

CHARLES ELME FRANCATELLI, *A Plain Cookery Book for the Working Classes*, 1852

PUDDING SAUCE

What we now think of as "custard" was often known as "pudding sauce"; set custards were eaten from a custard cup, like the one without a handle that, with two tumblers, comprises the Cratchits' "family display of glass." Catherine Dickens' menus often feature "custards," indicating different flavors. Eliza Acton suggests almonds, fruits, or liqueurs, or even a flavoring that hadn't yet gained its huge subsequent popularity—chocolate.

SERVES 6–8

4 organic free-range egg yolks

6½ tablespoons/80g golden caster sugar

1 teaspoon cornstarch/cornflour

2 cups plus 2 tablespoons/500ml full-fat/whole milk

½ teaspoon vanilla extract

Beat the egg yolks, sugar, and cornstarch/cornflour together until a pale gold color.

Warm the milk until just below boiling. Pour onto the egg yolk mixture, whisking all the time with a balloon whisk.

Return the mixture to the pan, add the vanilla extract, and heat very gently, stirring all the time with a wooden spoon until the mixture has the consistency of pouring cream. Don't let it boil or the eggs will separate.

Serve hot with puddings such as the Roly-Poly Jam Pudding (see page 139), Batter Pudding (page 136), or Christmas Pudding (page 106).

PUDDING SAUCE

Two teacupfuls of milk, half a cup of sugar, 2 eggs, and a tablespoonful of vanilla. Beat eggs to a froth with sugar. Boil milk and sugar, pour over them, stirring all the time; add vanilla.

PLAIN PUDDING SAUCE

One tablespoonful corn flour, large tablespoonful sugar, teacupful milk, and 1 egg.

Beat egg, sugar, and cornflour with tablespoonful of milk very light; boil the rest of the milk, pour it over the mixture stirring all the time.

MARTHA H. GORDON, *Cookery for Working Men's Wives*, 1888

CHAPTER 9

A Grand Occasion

Dombey and Son

— ◆ —

Coming Home from Church
H.K. Browne (Phiz)

The two grand feasts in *Dombey and Son* show why Dickens resisted the Victorian obsession with etiquette and display, and thought of formal parties with "unspeakable abhorrence" (letter, December 2, 1841). Unlike Jane Austen, for example, who pokes fun at those of her characters who concern themselves too much with food, Dickens is half-exasperated, half-amused by those who squander good food.

The stiff christening breakfast for baby Paul Dombey is ruined by the frostiness that defines Dombey senior's relationships. The "cold fowls-ham-patties-salad-lobster" and cold fillet of veal are delicious and elegant dishes, but there is a "toothache in everything" and nobody seems to eat. The contrast is provided by Uncle Sol and Walter who, eating a hot meal of expensive sole and steak to celebrate the beginning of their business career, ply their knives and forks with genuine hunger.

In the Dombeys' wedding feast, the food stands in for emotional substance. The principal actors don't care that "the pastry chef has done his duty like a man." The servants, catching the mood, carelessly down the champagne and treat the opulent "roast fowls, raised pies, and lobster salad" as "mere drugs." Dickens' description of the detritus of the feast is miserably comic: scraps, crumbs, spillages, and "pensive jellies, gradually resolving themselves into a lukewarm gummy soup." At the same time, the marriage of Dombey, who is determined that his wealth should ensure the submission of his bride, the impecunious and chilly Edith Granger, is "almost as denuded of its show and garnish as the breakfast."

In contrast to the Dombeys' wedding champagne, Uncle Sol keeps a valuable bottle of Madeira covered in dust and cobwebs, which is opened only once his family is complete again. In the sunshine "the golden wine within it sheds a lustre on the table"; and the clink of the family's glasses sounds like a "little peal of marriage bells," betokening a family that has finally found happiness.

~ RAISED PIE ~

The invention of the hinged pie mold enabled chefs to produce huge and elaborate pies, rather than raising them by hand, and no grand dinner, such as the Dombeys' wedding feast, would be complete without one. They were often waisted, which gave an elegant line and helped the filling to cook evenly. Although Mrs. Marshall gives a cold-water pastry, the traditional hot-water version will give your pie more stability.

SERVES 8–12

For the filling

1 lb 9 oz/700g chopped mixed game birds, such as pheasant, pigeon, partridge, wild duck (include some chicken if you find game very strong); also ask your butcher for the carcasses for the stock

8 oz/225g fresh pork belly, ground/minced

4 oz/115g unsmoked streaky bacon, very finely chopped

2 shallots, chopped

½ teaspoon ground mace

½ teaspoon ground allspice

½ teaspoon ground coralline (pink) peppercorns

¼ cup/60ml port or madeira

1 tablespoon freshly chopped parsley

2 hard-boiled egg yolks

1 teaspoon salt

50 small button mushrooms

½ cup/50g shelled pistachios

shavings of truffles (if available)

freshly ground black pepper

For the stock

bones and giblets from the carcasses

1 onion

1 carrot

1 celery stick

1 bay leaf

4 peppercorns

2–3 sprigs of thyme

4 leaves of gelatine

For the pastry

⅓ cup/75g cold, unsalted butter, diced

4 cups/550g strong white all-purpose/plain flour

¾ cup/200ml water

½ cup minus 1 tablespoon/100g lard

½ teaspoon salt

You will need an 8-inch/20-cm diameter springform cake pan/tin, approx. 3¼ inches/8 cm deep, greased with lard

Give yourself two days to make this pie.

To make the filling, mix all the meats together; add the chopped shallots, the spices and herbs, the port or madeira, and the egg yolks. Season with the salt and pepper, then mix in the button mushrooms and pistachios and, if using, truffle shavings. If possible, cover and leave overnight or for several hours for the flavors to develop.

Put the stock ingredients, except for the gelatine leaves, into a large pot, cover with cold water and bring to the boil. Skim it from time to time while it simmers, uncovered, until you have about 2½ cups/600ml liquid. Put it through a strainer/sieve.

When you are ready to make your pie, preheat the oven to 400°F/200°C/ Gas 6 and make the pastry. Rub the butter into the flour until it is the texture of fine breadcrumbs.

Warm the water, lard, and salt in a saucepan until the lard has melted and the liquid is nearly boiling. Tip it into the flour and mix together with a wooden spoon. Turn it out onto a floured surface and knead it quickly. Do not overhandle or it will become tough.

Roll out two-thirds of the pastry to line the greased cake pan/tin; use a little ball of pastry to push the pastry into the angles so it gives a clean line. Make sure there are no gaps or holes. Cut off the pastry level with the top of the pan/tin.

Fill the cake pan/tin with the meat mixture, allowing it to dome above the edges of the pan.

Roll out the remaining pastry to make a lid, punching out a small hole in the center. Wet the pastry at the top of the pie, place the lid on top, and pinch the edges together. Use the pastry trimmings to make leaves to decorate.

Bake in the preheated oven for 20 minutes, then turn down the oven to 350°F/180°C/Gas 4 and bake for another 1½ hours, covering with foil if the top starts to get too brown.

At the beginning of the pie's cooking time, soak the gelatine leaves in cold water for 8 minutes; squeeze out the excess water and dissolve the leaves in the warmed, strained stock.

Remove the pie from the oven, allow it to cool a little, then pour the cool liquid stock through the hole in the lid (use a funnel). Leave the pie in the cake pan/tin for a day before carefully taking it out.

FRENCH RAISED GAME PIE
PATE DE GIBIER A LA FRANÇAISE

Prepare a raised pie paste, and with it line a No. 2 size French raised pie mould to scarcely a quarter of an inch thick; then prepare a farce or mince as follows: Take ten ounces of veal, twelve ounces of fresh pork, and chop very fine, or pass twice through a mincing machine; season with coralline pepper, salt, and arrange this on the paste in the mould. Fill in with fillets of pigeon, chicken, or any game you may have, strips of tongue, ham, or bacon, hard-boiled yolks of eggs that are masked with chopped parsley and seasoned with pepper and salt, button mushrooms, pistachios, truffles, pâté de foie gras, cockscombs – and any farced birds, such as larks, quails, or ortolans, so as to stand higher than the mould; cover in with more of the farce or mince, and then put a somewhat thinner layer of paste over the top, first wetting the edges of the paste round the mould, press the edges together, and trim off the paste; brush the top lightly over with cold water, stamp out some rounds of the paste and work them into leaves or other pretty designs, and ornament the top of the pie with them; fix a buttered paper round the mould standing some six inches higher than the top of the pie.

Bake gently for about two and a half to three hours, taking care that the paste is not browned, as it should be a rich fawn colour when done; when cooked put the pie aside in the mould till it is cold, then remove the top by cutting the paste through round the edge of the mould, and fill up the pie with any nice meat jelly that is not quite set, and put aside again till the jelly is quite set; then cover the top with some chopped aspic and replace the paste cover. Remove the mould, dish on a paper, and it may be garnished round with aspic jelly. Care must be taken when filling up the mould that the jelly is not too liquid or it will go through the paste. This is excellent as a side dish, or for wedding breakfasts, ball suppers, and, in fact, for use generally.

RAISED PIE PASTE

Take one pound of fine flour and rub into it a quarter of a pound of butter, a pinch of salt, one whole egg, then mix it with cold water into a stiff paste and use.

MRS. A.B. MARSHALL'S *Cookery Book*, 1888

LOBSTER PATTIES

Paul Dombey's christening feast includes a "cold preparation of calf's head" which, though not uncommon on a grand table at the time, still has a tinge of the macabre, appropriate for this icy Dombey occasion where the food "cold fowls—ham—patties—salad—lobster" is luxurious but chilled. The Victorian patty (from the French for pastry) was a small version of the vol-au-vent case, which Eliza Acton commends as an elegant and economical way of using up leftovers.

MAKES 4 PATTIES

12 oz/350g ready-made puff pastry

1 cup/250ml fish or chicken stock

1 level dessertspoon all-purpose/plain flour

1 cup/250ml light/single cream

a few drops of lemon juice

1 cooked hen lobster, meat chopped and coral set aside

Preheat the oven to 400°F/200°C/Gas 6. Line a baking tray with baking parchment paper.

To make the pastry cases, roll out the pastry to ½ inch/12mm thick, taking care to keep it even so it rises evenly. Cut 2½-inch/6-cm circles and transfer them to the lined baking tray. Dip a 1¼-inch/3-cm cutter into very hot water and use it to cut halfway through the pastry. Bake in the preheated oven for 10–15 minutes until well risen and golden brown.

To make the lobster sauce, boil the stock to reduce it by half. In a bowl, mix the flour with a tablespoon of the cream, then stir in the rest of the cream. Gradually stir the warm stock into the cream mixture. Return it to the pan, add the lemon juice, and heat very gently, stirring all the time, for about 5 minutes, until it is a thick coating consistency. Take it off the heat. Crush the lobster coral (roe), add it to a tablespoon of the sauce, and beat them together well. Add this to the remainder of the white sauce and mix together. Add the chopped lobster meat.

Scoop out the lids of the patties using a sharp knife and trim the insides of the patties. Fill with the lobster sauce and serve warm.

This filling can be made with any fish or meat, using fish or meat stock as appropriate.

COMMON LOBSTER PATTIES

Prepare the fish as directed for fricasseed lobster, increasing a little the proportion of sauce. Fill the patty-cases with the mixture quite hot, and serve immediately.

Fricasseed Lobster: Take the flesh from the claws and tails of two moderate-sized lobsters, cut it into small scallops or dice; heat it slowly quite through in about three-quarters of a pint of good white sauce or béchamel; and serve it when it is at the point of boiling, after having stirred briskly to it a little lemon-juice just as it is taken from the fire.

Patty Cases: Roll out some of the lightest puff-paste to a half-inch of thickness, and with the larger of the tins cut the number of patties required; then dip the edge of the small shape into hot water, and press it about half through them. Bake them in a moderately quick oven from ten to twelve minutes, and when they are done, with the point of a sharp knife, take out the small rounds of crust from the tops, and scoop all the crumb from the inside of the patties, which may then be filled.

ELIZA ACTON, *Modern Cookery for Private Families*, 1845

CHARLOTTE RUSSE

Invented by the French chef Marie-Antoine Carême and quickly adopted
by aristocratic chefs, Charlotte Russe was a popular celebration dessert on
middle-class tables. *In What Shall We Have for Dinner?*, Catherine Dickens
has a recipe with Crème au Marasquin (a rich, set cream flavored with
liqueur made from maraschino cherries), whereas Theodore Garrett's recipe
adds a good, tart jelly and real fruit as a foil to the rich cream.

SERVES 10–12

1 batch (approx. 18) Ladies'
Fingers (see page 98)

2½ cups/600ml dark red liquid
jello/jelly (see Currant and \
Raspberry Jelly on page 154)

fresh fruit to decorate, such as
raspberries, strawberries,
cherries

For the crème

10 leaves of gelatine

2 scant cups/450ml full-fat/
whole milk

1 vanilla bean/pod

5 free-range egg yolks

2 level tablespoons caster sugar,
plus more to taste

3 cups/400g soft berries, puréed
(or you could use any stewed
and puréed fruit, such as

cherries, plums, apricots,
apples, gooseberries, or pears)

1 tablespoon fruit liqueur, such
as maraschino, framboise, or
cassis (optional)

scant 1¾ cups/400ml whipping
cream

You will need an 8¾-inch/22-cm
diameter springform cake pan/
tin. The setting takes several
hours, so give yourself plenty
of time.

To make the crème

Put the gelatine leaves into plenty of cold water to soak for
8–10 minutes. Put the milk in a saucepan with the vanilla bean/
pod, warm it without boiling, and let it infuse for 5 minutes. Whisk
the egg yolks and the sugar together in a bowl until thick and pale.

Remove the vanilla and heat the milk to just below boiling. Pour it
over the egg yolks and beat with a balloon whisk.

Squeeze excess water from the gelatine leaves and add the leaves to
the custard, then return it to the pan and heat very gently until it
thickens. Do not boil.

Let it cool a little, then fold in the fruit purée and, if you like, the
liqueur. When it is cold but not set, whip the cream and fold it into
the custard.

To assemble

Line the cake pan/tin with plastic wrap/clingfilm, then line the pan with the ladies' fingers, sugar side outermost, packing them together as tightly as possible (see page 98 about cutting them to fit).

Fill the center with the crème. Cover with plastic wrap/clingfilm and leave in the fridge to set. This will take at least 3–4 hours.

To add the jello/jelly

Start to make the jello/jelly (see page 154) about 3 hours before you want to add it, so that it is liquid but as cold as possible, without being set, so that it doesn't ooze through the sponge fingers.

You can either pour on half, let it set, then decorate with fruit and add the other half; or pour on all the jello/jelly, let it set, and decorate with fruit at the end. Give the jello/jelly at least another 3 hours in the fridge to set before unmolding.

To unmold

Place the springform pan on a stand so that you can unclip and pull down the outside of the pan. Using the plastic wrap/clingfilm lining, transfer the charlotte onto your serving plate. Cut the plastic wrap/clingfilm away from the sides, then ease it out from underneath. If you wish, tie a decorative ribbon around the sides of the dessert.

CHARLOTTE RUSSE

Put a little warmed jelly at the bottom of a plain round Charlotte-mould, pack it in ice, and when the jelly commences to set decorate that part of the mould with any fruit that may be desired. Pour in more of the warm jelly to cover the fruit and let it set firm. Cut a few savoy biscuits into various shapes, dip them in sweet jelly, and decorate the sides of the mould with them. Put ½ lb of ripe strawberry puree or jam into a basin, and mix in 1 pint of sweet cream and 1oz of dissolved gelatine. Pour this mixture into the cavity in the mould, cover the top over with a tin, pack ice on the top, and let it remain until the whole is set and firm. Turn the Charlotte out of the mould when ready, and serve.

THEODORE GARRETT, *The Encyclopaedia of Practical Cookery, Volume 3*, 1892-94

ORANGE AND REDCURRANT JELLIES

Victorian jelly-making was elaborate. The jellies (jello) for Mr. and Mrs.
Dombey's ill-starred wedding breakfast were glamorous and grown-up party
pieces, not like today's commercial ones served as children's party food.
Francatelli's recipes for "oranges filled with transparent jelly" and his striped
or "Panachee" jelly are the perfect way to serve orange jelly (which he tints
pink with cochineal) and currant and raspberry jelly.

SERVES 4–6

For the orange jelly

7 oranges

½ cup/100g granulated
sugar

⅔ cup/150ml cold
water

orange juice from a
carton (if required)

7 sheets platinum grade
gelatine

You will need a jelly bag
or muslin

Orange Jelly

Halve six oranges, gently squeeze out most of the juice with a squeezer,
and set aside.

Remove the white pith and remaining pulp from the halved oranges using
a teaspoon or grapefruit spoon, taking care not to damage the peel. Do
not remove the stalk or you'll have a little hole; if you get this, plug it with
kitchen paper. Set the 12 orange halves in muffin pans to keep them level.

Make the orange jelly. Pare the rind from the remaining orange, making
sure you have just orange rind and no white pith; then squeeze this and
add the juice to the rest. Gently heat the sugar and water together until
you have a syrup; don't let it boil. Add the orange rind and leave to cool
until it is lukewarm.

Meanwhile, squeeze or liquidize the orange pulp (if you liquidize it,
make sure you've taken all the pips out first) to extract all the juice, then
discard the pulp. Measure the total amount of orange juice—you will need
2½ cups/600ml so add more orange juice from a carton if necessary.

Soak the gelatine leaves in cold water until they have swollen and gone
wrinkly (about 6–8 minutes, but no more than 10 minutes or the gelatine
starts to disintegrate; also make sure that the leaves don't stick together).

Remove the orange rind from the cooled syrup; add the juice to the syrup
in the pan and heat very gently to lukewarm. Squeeze the excess water
from the gelatine leaves, add them to the pan of juice and syrup, and stir
until dissolved. Let the mixture cool until it is nearly cold but not set.

Pour the cooled orange jelly into six of the orange halves. Leave in the
fridge for several hours to set, or in the freezer for about an hour. When
the jelly is completely set, cut each half into quarters. Trim off any excess
rind with scissors.

For the currant and raspberry jelly

**5 cups/500g redcurrants and
4 cups/500g raspberries, or
2 lb 3 oz/1kg red or black fruit**

⅔ cup/150ml cold water

**6½–8 tablespoons/80–100g
granulated sugar (add another
4 tablespoons/50g for dark fruit
and taste throughout)**

**approx. 6 leaves of platinum
grade gelatine**

Currant and Raspberry Jelly

You can make this with any combination of fruit following some rules. Keep red fruits separate from black. Strawberries and raspberries do not need cooking— just adding them to the hot liquid should make them soft enough to squeeze the juice out. Redcurrants, blackcurrants, blackberries, red and black plums (quartered and stoned), and cherries do need some cooking with sugar and water.

Simmer the currants with the water and sugar for 20–30 minutes. Add the raspberries to the hot liquid, pressing them to get the juice out. Add more sugar to taste. Let it cool and then let it drip through a jelly bag or muslin into a bowl, keeping the juice and discarding the pulp (it will take about an hour).

Measure the juice and for every 7 tablespoons/100ml of liquid, use 1 leaf of gelatine. Soak the gelatine in cold water for 6–8 minutes, as on page 153.

Meanwhile, warm the juice to lukewarm; squeeze the excess water out of the gelatine leaves and add them to the liquid. When they have dissolved completely, let the mixture cool until it is nearly cold but not set.

Pour the cool red jelly into the remaining six orange halves. Leave to set as above, then cut each into quarters and trim as on page 153. Serve the red and orange jellies in alternating colors on a plate.

To Make Panachee Jelly

Any remaining liquid can be set as stripes in a small jelly mold; the easiest way to do this is to pour in the first layer and put it into the freezer until ice crystals just form on the top.

Add the next layer of cooled jelly (if it has solidified, you can warm it again, but don't layer it until it is cool or you won't get a nice sharp line between the two colors).

Let the jellies set in the fridge for several hours or overnight (or in the freezer if you are really short of time, but don't let them freeze).

Turn the jelly out by dipping the mold briefly in warm water (not too long or the jelly will start to melt), then clamping a plate on top and inverting it.

ORANGES FILLED WITH TRANSPARENT JELLY

Select half a dozen oranges without specks on the rind, make a hole at the stalk-end with a circular tin cutter, about half an inch in diameter, and then use a small teaspoon to remove all the pulp and loose pitch from the interior; when this is effected, soak the oranges in cold water for about an hour, then introduce the spoon through the aperture, and scrape the insides smooth, and after rincing them again in cold water, set them to drain on a cloth.

Next, stop up any holes that may have been made in them while scooping out the pulp, and set the oranges in some pounded rough ice contained in a deep sautapan; fill three of them with bright pink-orange jelly, and the remainder with plain jelly. When the jelly has become firm, wipe the oranges with a clean cloth, cut each into four quarters, dish them up tastefully on an ornamental pastry-stand, or upon a napkin, and send to table.

CHARLES ELME FRANCATELLI, *The Modern Cook*, 1846

CURRANT AND RASPBERRY JELLY

Pick the stalks from one quart of redcurrants and a pottle of raspberries, then put these into a large basin with half a pound of pounded sugar and a gill of spring water. Bruise them thoroughly, by squeezing them with the back part of the bowl of a wooden spoon against the sides of the basin. Then throw the whole into a beaver jelly bag, and filter the juice, pouring it back into the bag until it runs through perfectly bright. Next add half a pint of clarified syrup, and two ounces of clarified isinglass to the juice, and pour the jelly into a mould placed in rough ice to receive it.

CHARLES ELME FRANCATELLI, *The Modern Cook*, 1846

~ ITALIAN CREAM ~

Dickens, convalescing after surgery, wrote to Angela Burdett-Coutts that his legs were like "tremulous Italian cream." Most Victorian creams were set with isinglass in molds and wobbled like jelly. Catherine's unusual recipe doesn't use a setting agent, but is a marriage of lemon syllabub and cream cheese. Sadly, her critics have derided her fondness for this luscious dessert and her plumpness.

1⅛ cups/250g mascarpone or full-fat cream cheese

1⅔ cups/400ml thick heavy/double cream

zest of 1–2 lemons

⅓–¾ cup/50–100g confectioner's/icing sugar

juice of ½ lemon

2 tablespoons sweet white wine, such as white Vin Santo

berries, herbs, or edible flowers to decorate

Beat the mascarpone or cream cheese in a large bowl until smooth, then add the cream, half the lemon zest, and half the sugar, followed by the lemon juice and wine.

Stir well to combine; add more zest or sugar to taste. Whisk until the cream mixture forms soft peaks.

Spoon into a serving bowl or individual glasses and decorate with berries, sprigs of mint, flowering herbs such as rosemary, bergamot, or borage, or edible flowers such as calendula or violas. Serve with the jellies on pages 153–54, or with the Homemade Biscuits on page 97.

ITALIAN CREAM

Whip together for nearly an hour a quart of very thick scalded cream, a quart of raw cream, the grated rind of four lemons and the strained juice, with ten ounces of white powdered sugar, then add half-a-pint of sweet wine, and continue to whisk it until it becomes quite solid; lay a piece of muslin in a sieve, and ladle the cream upon it with a spoon; in twenty hours turn it carefully out, but mind it does not break; garnish it with fruit, jelly, or with flowers.

CATHERINE DICKENS, *What Shall We Have for Dinner?*, 1851

CHAPTER 10

Drinks with Dickens

The Pickwick Papers

— ◆ —

Mr. Pickwick in the Pound
H.K. Browne (Phiz)

The Pickwick Papers, written when Dickens was in his early twenties, is a jubilant cocktail of drinks, dissipation, and hangovers. Its traveling heroes go from inn to inn—The Angel at Bury, The Great White Horse in Ipswich, The George and Vulture in the City of London. Mr. Tupman, fancying himself suicidally broken-hearted, flees to The Leather Bottle in Cobham, Kent (which is still there), and revives himself with roast fowl, bacon, and ale. The friends leave Mr. Pickwick in a wheelbarrow, sleeping off his picnic and cold punch on a hot day. They celebrate with the old-fashioned "wassail"—warm ale or hard cider and roast apples—at Mr. Wardle's Manor Farm Christmas. Sam Weller drinks expensive, gentlemanly brandy, reflecting his aspiration to "be a gen'l'm'n myself one of these days."

Mr. Micawber, downcast by his latest financial woes, is transformed by the fragrance of lemon peel and sugar, burning rum and steam as he makes the company a bowl of punch in *David Copperfield*. Dickens believed that poor people were just as entitled to enjoy a drink as the wealthy, and that drunkenness was a symptom rather than a cause of poverty. The broken cask of wine in *A Tale of Two Cities* leads to a "special companionship" among those who rush to enjoy its "miraculous presence." Dickens mocks the teetotal movement through Sam Weller's exposure of the hypocrisy and self-interest of the "United Grand Junction Ebenezer Temperance Association." Hogarthian disapproval of working-class drinking is rare in Dickens but he is not blind to its problems—in his "Seven Dials" (*Sketches by Boz*), he describes a brawl between ladies drunk on "gin-and-bitters."

Pickwick Clubs—some drinking clubs, some earnest proponents of social reform—have been founded in London, New Orleans, and all over the world, in honor of Dickens and his most exuberant book.

～ WASSAIL ～

The revelers at Old Wardle's sat down to a "mighty bowl of wassail," an old country drink of hot ale, often thickened with eggs and with roasted apples bobbing in it. It was a drink for Christmas, New Year, or Twelfth Night, particularly in orchard counties, where revelers toasted the apple trees with wassail to bless the new year's crops. Since modern beers become bitter when heated, cider is a good substitute.

SERVES 6-8

1 quart/1 litre strong dry hard cider or scrumpy

2-4 tablespoons brown sugar, according to taste

2-3 tablespoons apple brandy, or more to taste

6 cloves

2 cinnamon sticks

1 small piece of ginger

a little grated nutmeg, or some small pieces of nutmeg

orange and lemon slices

Put all the ingredients into a saucepan and heat very gently for 15-20 minutes. Do not allow the mixture to boil.

When you are ready to serve, fish out the spices and fruit with a strainer/sieve or slotted spoon, then pour the liquid into heatproof cups.

WASSAIL

(This version is called Brown Betty by Richard Cook)

Dissolve a quarter of a pound of brown sugar in one pint of water, slice a lemon into it, let it stand a quarter of an hour, then add a small quantity of pulverized cloves and cinnamon, half a pint of brandy, and one quart of good strong ale; stir it well together, put a couple of slices of toasted bread into it, grate some nutmeg and ginger on the toast, and it is fit for use.

RICHARD COOK, *Oxford Night Caps: A Collection of Receipts for Making Various Beverages Used in the University*, 1827

CURRANT WINE

In Dickens' time, few people could afford French wine, so they made their own from oranges or hedgerow fruits and flowers, such as cowslips, elder, sloes, and blackberries. Red, white, or blackcurrants cropped prolifically in moist, cool English gardens and made a simple country wine, although, as Martin Chuzzlewit found at his Installation Banquet, it could be acidic. This version, made with brandy, is smooth and comparatively quick to make. It was also known as "currant shrub."

MAKES 25–33 FL OZ/
750ML–1 LITRE

2 lb 3 oz/1kg redcurrants, blackcurrants, blueberries, or raspberries, washed

17 fl oz/500ml brandy

1¾–2½ cups/350–500g granulated sugar

You will need a 50-fl oz/1.5-litre wide-necked glass or plastic container with a good lid, jelly bag or 2 squares of muslin, and screw-top wine bottles or preserving bottles (such as Kilner) with a good seal

Sterilize the container—either wash in hot, soapy water, then place in a pan of boiling water and simmer for 10 minutes, or use a sterilizing tablet (these usually take 15–30 minutes to work, but follow the manufacturer's instructions)—and rinse well.

Put the washed fruit in your container and mash well with a potato masher. Add the brandy and mix together, then close the lid tightly. Leave in a cool, dark place for 1–2 months, turning the jar from time to time to keep it well mixed.

When you are ready to strain the wine, sterilize the jelly bag by placing it in a pan of water with a little soap powder, bringing it to the boil, and leaving it to cool, or use a sterilizing tablet. Alternatively, use a double layer of clean muslin squares in a strainer/sieve.

Suspend the jelly bag or place the strainer/sieve over a clean container (a large pitcher/jug with a lip is best). Pour in the fruit and liquid and leave it for a few hours to drip through. When it has stopped dripping, squeeze the bag or use the back of a spoon to get the last of the juice out.

Add the sugar to taste. Start with the smaller quantity as you can add more later.

Return the liquid to the large container and leave for a couple of weeks, shaking it every now and again to encourage the sugar to dissolve. After a week or two, taste and add more sugar if you wish, then leave for a few more days.

If the wine is cloudy, filter it again. Then decant it into sterilized bottles or Kilner jars. You can use it immediately, but it improves after some months. Enjoy it as a liqueur or use it like cassis and add to white or sparkling wine.

RASPBERRY OR CURRANT WINE

Put five quarts of currants, and a pint of raspberries, to every two gallons of water; let them soak a night; then squeeze and break them well. Next day rub them well on a fine wire sieve, till all the juice is obtained, washing the skins again with some of the water; then to every gallon put four pounds of very good Lisbon sugar, but not white, which is often adulterated; turn it immediately, and lay the bung lightly on. Do not use any thing to work it. In two or three days put a bottle of brandy to every four gallons; bung it close, but leave the peg out at top a few days; keep it three years and it will be a very fine agreeable wine; four years would make it still better.

MRS. RUNDELL, *A New System of Domestic Cookery*, 1806

~~ PINEAPPLE RUM ~~

Dickens mocked the temperance movement through the Reverend Mr.
Stiggins, who preached abstinence yet drank pineapple rum. Dickens enjoyed
the drink himself: there were "5 dozen fine old Pine Apple Rum" in his cellar
at Gad's Hill in Kent. Inspired by Revd. Stiggins, pineapple rum is again
made commercially, by steeping the rind and flesh of pineapples in separate
rum casks for some months. Cedric Dickens, great-grandson of Charles,
offers an easier version.

1 pineapple

sugar

1 bottle dark rum

Use this as a base for punch or
serve with fruit juices, such as
pineapple, orange, or cranberry,
or with coconut milk.

MR. STIGGINS' PINEAPPLE RUM

*Slice a pineapple very thinly, sprinkle with
a little sugar and leave for a day. Set aside two
slices and press the juice out of the rest, adding
to it an equal amount of sweetened rum
(two oz sugar to half a pint rum). Put into
a jar with the spare slices of pineapple.
Leave, well stoppered, for three weeks.
Strain and bottle.*

CEDRIC DICKENS, *Drinking with Dickens*, 1980

A PUNCH FOR TWO CITIES

"Those were drinking days and most men drank hard", Dickens writes
of his two lawyers in *A Tale of Two Cities*. A kettle and the ingredients for
hot punch—brandy, rum, sugar, and lemons—are on the table in Stryver's
chambers. Dickens' favorite drink betokens warmth, cheer, and confidences,
even between "the Lion," Stryver, and his guest, "the Jackal,"
the dissipated Sydney Carton.

SERVES 10–12

peel and juice of 3 unwaxed
lemons

5½ oz/150g brown sugar cubes

1⅔ cups/400ml good-quality
Jamaican rum

1 cup plus 1 tablespoon/250ml
Cognac

4½ cups/1 litre boiling water

You will need a large enamel
pan with a lid

Carefully peel the lemons, not including the bitter white pith. Place
in the pan and add the sugar, rum, and brandy. Warm gently.

Take a metal ladleful of the warm spirit, set it alight using a long
match and holding it over the pan, then carefully pour the flaming
liquid back into the pan to inflame the rest of the liquid.

Let the spirits in the pan burn for 3–4 minutes, then extinguish the
flame by putting the lid on. If you don't like the idea of flaming
spirits in your kitchen, warm the punch to just below boiling and let
it simmer for a few minutes to evaporate some of the alcohol.

Add the lemon juice and the boiling water. Let it cool for 5 minutes;
taste for sugar and add more if desired. Leave to stand for 15
minutes in a warm place or a low oven. Discard the pieces of lemon
peel before ladling the punch into heatproof glasses.

DICKENS' PUNCH

To Mrs Fillonneau,

48, Rue de Courcelles, Eighteenth January, 1847

My Dear Mrs F.

I send you, on the other side, the tremendous document which will make you for ninety years (I hope) a beautiful Punchmaker in more senses than one.

I shall be delighted to dine with you on Thursday. Mr Forster says amen. Commend me to your Lord, and believe me (with respectful compliment to Lord Chesterfield) always,

Faithfully yours,

Charles Dickens

TO MAKE THREE PINTS OF PUNCH

Peel into a very strong common basin (which may be broken, in case of accident, without damage to the owner's peace or pocket) the rinds of three lemons, cut very thin, and with as little as possible of the white coating between the peel and the fruit, attached. Add a double-handfull of lump sugar (good measure), a pint of good old rum, and a large wine-glass full of brandy – if it be not a large claret glass, say two. Set this on fire, by filling a warm silver spoon with the spirit, lighting the contents at a wax taper, and pouring them gently in. Let it burn three or four minutes at least, stirring it from time to time. Then extinguish it by covering the basin with a tray, which will immediately put out the flame. Then squeeze in the juice of the three lemons, and add a quart of boiling water. Stir the whole well, cover it up for five minutes, and stir again.

At this crisis (having skimmed off the lemon pips with a spoon) you may taste. If not sweet enough add sugar to your liking, but observe that it will be a little sweeter presently. Pour the whole into a jug, tie a leather or coarse cloth over the top, so as to exclude the air completely, and stand it in a hot oven ten minutes, or on a hot stove one quarter of an hour. Keep it until it comes to table in a warm place near the fire, but not too hot. If it be intended to stand three or four hours, take half the lemon-peel out, or it will acquire a bitter taste.

The same punch allowed to grow cool by degrees, and then iced, is delicious. It requires less sugar when made for this purpose. If you wish to produce it bright, strain it into bottles through silk.

The proportions and directions will, of course, apply to any quantity.

MINT JULEP

A julep was an old country cordial (Milton refers to it in *Comus*) of mint and honey and other spirits. The Americans perfected it as a cocktail with bourbon; on his trip there, Dickens drank mint juleps all evening with Washington Irving and Philip Hone. He seems to have preferred the gin version he had later, describing it in a letter written on March 21, 1844, as "the most deliciously cunning compound that ever I tasted; nectar could not stand before it; Jupiter would have hobnobbed in it."

SERVES 1

6–8 mint leaves, ideally spearmint

2–3 teaspoons sugar syrup or runny honey

3½ tablespoons/50ml (large shot glass) brandy, bourbon (American whiskey), or gin

crushed ice and a sprig of mint, to serve

Juleps are traditionally served in a metal cup which you hold by the base or handle, so the outside frosts up. If possible, leave the alcohol and metal cups in the freezer for a few hours or days.

Gently press the mint leaves in the sugar syrup or honey—not too hard or you may get a bitter taste. Pour over the spirit.

Put crushed ice into a glass or metal cup, pour the liquid over, and stir to get frost on the outside of the cup. Serve with a sprig of mint.

MINT JULEP (AN AMERICAN RECIPE)

Strip the tender leaves of mint into a tumbler, and add to them as much wine, brandy, or any other spirit, as you wish to take. Put some pounded ice into a second tumbler, pour this on the mint and brandy, and continue to pour the mixture from one tumbler to the other until the whole is sufficiently impregnated with the flavor of the mint, which is extracted by the particles of the ice coming into brisk contact when changed from one vessel to the other. Now place the glass in a larger one, containing pounded ice; on taking it out of which it will be covered with frost-work.

SARAH JOSEPHA HALE, *The Ladies' New Book of Cookery*, 1852

~ SMOKING BISHOP ~

Scrooge tells Bob Cratchit that they will discuss his affairs over a bowl of
"Smoking Bishop," a drink chosen over the more common punch (like turkey
in preference to goose) because, made with port, it connotes wealth
and fine living. The drink was also known as Oxford Bishop; other
versions termed Cardinal and Pope substituted (respectively) claret
and champagne for the port.

SERVES 6–8

1 whole orange or lemon

16 whole cloves

2 cups plus 2 tablespoons/500ml
water

1–2 tablespoons soft brown
sugar, or to taste

1 cinnamon stick

2–3 blades of mace

6 allspice berries

¾–1¼-inch/2–3-cm cube of
ginger root, peeled

3¼ cups/750-ml bottle of ruby
port

juice of ½ an orange or lemon

a little grated nutmeg

Preheat the oven to 400°F/200°C/Gas 6.

Stud the orange or lemon with the cloves and roast it on a baking
tray for 20–30 minutes until soft. Don't let it go brown.

Meanwhile, put the water, sugar, and spices into a pan, bring to the
boil, then simmer until the water has reduced by half. Add the port,
lemon or orange juice, and a little grated nutmeg to taste; heat
without boiling.

Serve in a punch bowl with the clove-studded orange or lemon and
the spices floating in it.

SMOKING BISHOP

Make several incisions in the rind of a lemon, stick cloves in the incisions, and roast the lemon by a slow fire. Put small but equal quantities of cinnamon, cloves, mace, and all-spice, and a race of ginger, into a saucepan, with half a pint of water; let it boil until it is reduced one half. Boil one bottle of port wine; burn a portion of the spirit out of it, by applying a lighted paper to the saucepan. Put the roasted lemon and spice into the wine; stir it up well, and let it stand near the fire ten minutes. Rub a few knobs of sugar on the rind of a lemon, put the sugar into a bowl or jug, with the juice of half a lemon (not roasted), pour the wine upon it, grate some nutmeg into it, sweeten it to your taste, and serve it up with the lemon and spice floating in it.

Oranges, although not used in Bishop at Oxford, are, as will appear by the following lines written by Swift, sometimes introduced into that beverage:

Fine oranges
Well roasted, with sugar and wine in a cup,
They'll make a sweet Bishop when gentlefolks sup.

RICHARD COOK, *Oxford Night Caps: A Collection of Receipts for Making Various Beverages Used in the University*, 1827

BIBLIOGRAPHY

Cookbooks

I have given the original publication date for each book, although recipes may have been taken from later editions.

Acton, Eliza, *Modern Cookery for Private Families*, 1845

Anon, Eighteenth-century manuscript recipe book, National Library of Scotland, http://digital.nls.uk/107325984

Beeton, Isabella, *The Book of Household Management*, 1861

Cook, Richard, *Oxford Night Caps: A Collection of Receipts for Making Various Beverages Used in the University*, 1827

Dickens, Catherine, pseud. Lady Maria Clutterbuck, *What Shall We Have for Dinner?*, 1851

Dickens, Cedric, *Drinking with Dickens*, 1980

Farley, John, *The London Art of Cookery*, 1783

Francatelli, Charles Elmé, *The Cook's Guide, and Housekeeper's and Butler's Assistant*, 1861

Francatelli, Charles Elmé, *The Modern Cook*, 1846

Francatelli, Charles Elmé, *A Plain Cookery Book for the Working Classes*, 1852

Garrett, Theodore Francis, ed., *The Encyclopaedia of Practical Cookery* (8 volumes), 1892–94

Glasse, Hannah, *The Art of Cookery Made Plain and Easy*, 1747

Gordon, Martha H., *Cookery for Working Men's Wives*, 1888

Hale, Sarah Josepha Buell, *The Ladies' New Book of Cookery*, 1852

Hartley, Dorothy, *Food in England*, 1954

Johnstone, Christian Isobel, pseud. Margaret Dods, *The Cook and Housewife's Manual*, 1826

Kitchiner, William, *Apicius Redivivus, or The Cook's Oracle*, 1817

Marshall, Agnes B., *Mrs A.B. Marshall's Cookery Book*, 1888

Morton, D.O., in *Melrose Household Treasure*, 1877

Rundell, Maria Eliza, *A New System of Domestic Cookery*, 1806

Soyer, Alexis, *Charitable Cookery*, 1847

Soyer, Alexis, *The Gastronomic Regenerator*, 1846

Soyer, Alexis, *The Modern Housewife or Ménagère*, 1849

Soyer, Alexis, *The Poor Man's Regenerator*, 1848

Soyer, Alexis, *A Shilling Cookery for the People*, 1854

Suggested reading

Dickens, Cedric, *Dining with Dickens*, 1984

The Dickensian, published by the Dickens Fellowship.

Mayhew, Henry, *London Labour and the London Poor* (3 volumes), 1851

Nayder, Lillian, *The Other Dickens: A Life of Catherine Hogarth*, 2010

Rossi-Wilcox, Susan, *Dinner for Dickens: The Culinary History of Mrs Charles Dickens' Menu Books*, 2005

Tomalin, Claire, *Charles Dickens: A Life*, 2011

Charles Dickens' works

Sketches by Boz, 1836

The Pickwick Papers, 1837

Oliver Twist, 1839

Nicholas Nickleby, 1839

The Old Curiosity Shop, 1841

Barnaby Rudge, 1841

American Notes, 1842

A Christmas Carol, 1843

Martin Chuzzlewit, 1844

Pictures from Italy, 1846

Dombey and Son, 1848

David Copperfield, 1850

Bleak House, 1853

Hard Times, 1854

Little Dorrit, 1857

A Tale of Two Cities, 1859

Great Expectations, 1861

Mrs Lirriper's Legacy, 1864

Our Mutual Friend, 1865

The Uncommercial Traveller, 1869

The Mystery of Edwin Drood, 1870

Household Words (ed.), 1850–59

The Letters of Charles Dickens, The British Academy/The Pilgrim Edition, 12 volumes, eds Madeline House and Graham Storey

INDEX

ACKNOWLEDGMENTS

My great thanks to the friends and family who helped me with ideas and
editing, recipes, and testing: Margaret Bluman, Isabelle de Cat, Annabel
Huxley, Eleanor Koss, Robbie Koss, David Marshall, Claire McElwee, Simone
Doctors, Miranda Vogler-Koss, and particularly my mum, Jill Vogler.

Thank you to Louisa Price and Frankie Kubicki at the Charles Dickens
Museum for their help and interest. Thanks, too, to the talented team at
CICO Books, particularly Sally Powell, and Cindy Richards, Penny Craig, and
Patricia Harrington; to Gillian Haslam for her editing; and to Ria Osborne,
Luis Peral, and Ellie Jarvis for the food photography.

PICTURE CREDITS